MISCARRIED
Souls

Lorraine Elizabeth Stone

BALBOA.
PRESS

A DIVISION OF HAY HOUSE

Balboa Press books may be ordered through booksellers or by contacting:

Balboa Press
A Division of Hay House
1663 Liberty Drive
Bloomington, IN 47403
www.balboapress.com.au
1 (877) 407-4847

Because of the dynamic nature of the Internet, any web addresses or links contained in this book may have changed since publication and may no longer be valid. The views expressed in this work are solely those of the author and do not necessarily reflect the views of the publisher, and the publisher hereby disclaims any responsibility for them.

The author of this book does not dispense medical advice or prescribe the use of any technique as a form of treatment for physical, emotional, or medical problems without the advice of a physician, either directly or indirectly. The intent of the author is only to offer information of a general nature to help you in your quest for emotional and spiritual well-being. In the event you use any of the information in this book for yourself, which is your constitutional right, the author and the publisher assume no responsibility for your actions.

Any people depicted in stock imagery provided by Thinkstock are models, and such images are being used for illustrative purposes only.
Certain stock imagery © Thinkstock.

Print information available on the last page.

ISBN: 978-1-5043-0865-6 (sc)
ISBN: 978-1-5043-0866-3 (e)

Balboa Press rev. date: 06/21/2017

For every parent whose child grew wings, and for all of your precious angels.

CONTENTS

INTRODUCTION

Miscarriage and stillbirth are, even in this day and age, commonly treated as highly taboo words. Something best ignored and swept under the carpet so as to avoid causing any upset or embarrassment to others. I have studied numerous testimonies from women whose feelings and concerns have been cruelly dismissed because their loss was somehow deemed less important, less valid, than other losses.

This widespread apathy absolutely saddened and angered me in equal measures. I desperately wanted to shake the denial and flippant behaviour from those dishing out the silence. I wanted to shout out from the rooftops, to force people to listen and to acknowledge grieving mothers and fathers everywhere!

Reluctantly, however, I conceded that society as a whole has a long way to go before my suggestions will carry any weight or sway people to relinquish their deep rooted beliefs. Instead, I decided to devote time to supporting those who mattered most, the grieving parents themselves.

The message I really want to convey through my writing is that no matter how short a baby's life in the womb, life is still life, and every little life is precious. People will ask us why we get so hung up on a child that didn't get to take an earthly breath and for these folk no explanation will ever satisfy.

Our beautiful babies are our most treasured gifts, and nothing could ever replace them. Equally, there is absolutely nothing that could ever suppress the overwhelming, all-encompassing love that we feel for them. No woman should be made to feel that her loss is irrelevant, ever! A bereaved mother is, and will eternally be, a mother to each and every angel she has conceived.

My second aim is to reassure those suffering from the shock and agony of what can only be described as enduring the worst torture imaginable, that your little ones are completely safe and well, even those lost at the very earliest gestation.

Through channelled readings via mediums, my miscarried son Kieran has presented messages of comfort and hope from the afterlife. By sharing his thought provoking words and experiences, my intention is to offer reassurance to any parent questioning what may have become of their lost baby and to reveal that not only are your little ones blissfully content but that they have never actually been lost at all. They are still very much with you and always will be.

PART ONE
THE DARKEST DAYS

Chapter One

THE UNSPEAKABLE LOSS

How very softly you tiptoed into our world,
almost silently.

Only a moment, you stayed. But what an
imprint your footprints have left on our hearts

– Dorothy Ferguson

Miscarriage and stillbirth have always been considered
inconvenient subjects, and this type of loss is one that
leaves many people struggling to comprehend and to
voice genuinely supportive and sensitive words of comfort
towards. Yes, we have come a long way since the time of our
grandmothers and great-grandmothers when the experience
was really something that one didn't talk about. The very
British 'stiff upper lip' seemed to be the order of the day.

Women suffering the heartache of giving birth to a
stillborn baby were, in the past, instructed that there was

no need to see or to hold their child and no need to ask such vital and natural a question as "Is it a girl or a boy?" It was generally agreed that the less fuss made, the sooner mother would recover from the experience. Babies were buried in communal graves, and often the sex of the baby was not recorded.

Thankfully the need to express emotion has now been recognised as a vital part of the healing process and women are encouraged to open up and to speak about their tragic losses. Babies born still in many hospitals today are no longer whisked away, and parents are invited to hold their little angels and to spend precious time with them. Sleeping babies can be placed in specially adapted cots so that parents are able to say goodbye over a longer period of time. Photographs can be taken, and little hand and foot casts made by visiting specialists. Sadly, services such as these are still not available in every hospital, however.

Support groups, counselling and social media forums are now more readily available, and it can be extremely helpful for women and men to be put in contact with others who have experienced the same trauma. (I have listed some useful organisations in New Zealand, Australia, the UK and US in the pages at the back of the book.)

Vast improvements have been made over the years, but I believe that there is still a very long way to go towards ensuring that every family is able to obtain the dignity and assistance, not to mention the compassion, required at this devastating time.

Many parents enduring the ravages of miscarriage and stillbirth before the baby has reached twenty weeks in some countries, and twenty-four weeks in most, are unable to register their child which is absolutely heartbreaking! Thankfully, many baby loss support groups are helping to rectify this in a small way by offering parents specially made (unofficial) certificates on which baby's name and details can be added, and each little life remembered.

I cannot imagine having to endure the agonising process of birthing an angel baby, of raising a little one to childhood, or even into adulthood and then having them snatched away from me, it must induce the most excruciating pain imaginable, I feel for any parent who has had to suffer this. Because of my unusual 'back to front' experience, I have frequently questioned my right to comment on this type of loss, worrying that I might offend and irritate, which could not be further from my intention.

Although I was not fully aware that I had miscarried my son at the time, and because my grief was delayed as a result, the situation I find myself in is completely different to the majority of women. I do not pretend for one moment to have suffered the same impact that these incredibly brave women have.

Once my child had been acknowledged, I was finally able to begin my unconventional journey through the grief process. Despite having had a dissimilar experience to most, I wholeheartedly understand the incessant *what if's* and *what might have been's,* and my words are shared with the deepest of respect, from one mother to another.

Losing a baby is like losing a limb, a part of the mother passes with her child. All of the dreams and expectations, the milestones we will never get to see our baby reach, the wondering what he would have looked like, which activities he would have enjoyed taking part in and a thousand more unanswered questions are never far from our thoughts.

Because our babies passed before they had the chance to experience an earthly life outside of the womb, many presume that our grief should be less pronounced. I have heard countless insensitive comments, made in passing, around miscarriage, in particular, suggesting that a woman who never got to meet her infant somehow deserves less sympathy, because she hadn't had the chance to bond with her child. This is of course absolutely ridiculous! Ask any woman with the intense desire to become a mother, who has discovered the joy of becoming pregnant, and she will tell you that within hours of receiving this fantastic, life changing news, she will have made endless plans. Her due date will have been calculated, along with a compilation of possible first and middle names. Dreams are already being made, and these extend way into the future!

Mothers losing a baby early into a pregnancy may have nothing more than a plastic pregnancy test to remember their child by, some may not even have this. I would give anything to have a photograph or similar treasure to remember my son by. The longing to hold him in my arms is persistent, and I feel that these basic natural needs are so often cruelly disregarded, particularly around very early loss. Every woman who has lost a baby deserves to have her feelings, and her little one acknowledged - no matter how briefly she carried her precious child for.

Insensitive comments such as "Oh well, at least you can have another one," however well intended, are unhelpful and frankly horrendously hurtful. We don't want another one, we wanted *this* one! And very sadly, some women may not get the opportunity to 'have another one.' How anybody can imagine that one child may simply be replaced by another, I find completely unfathomable. We are not talking about replacing a broken plate here. This was our baby, our future toddler, child, young adult and so very much more.

For those of us who are lucky enough to have gone on to have subsequent children, Rainbow babies as they are often lovingly referred to because they depict the bright promise of hope after the storm, the frequently heard "Well at least you've got another one" is also cruel. Yes, we realise that we are very lucky to have experienced an entirely different, positive outcome this time around, but that doesn't mean that we are ready to throw all thoughts and emotions connected to our lost baby out of the window or to disown them and their memory.

I feel that there should be much more education around grief and the notion that we are sad for a little while, and then get back to 'normal,' whatever normal means. After losing a loved one, our *normal* will never be the same again.

Instead, we work towards a new normality, one in which we eventually learn to step forward, carrying the memory of our lost child with us. Nobody has the right to dictate when this should happen.

The journey through grief is a very personal one and is something that we move through at our own unique pace, which is as it should be. Just as an older loved one is remembered, the mother of an angel should also be able to honour her lost baby for as long as she chooses to do so, without being made to feel uncomfortable and without the expectation that she should have 'moved on' or be 'over it' by now. It doesn't matter if a woman lost her baby at four weeks, four months or if her loss occurred four decades ago, she is still a mother and will always be a mother.

I know that my son will be in my thoughts and in my heart until the day I pass and finally get to hold him. I don't feel stuck, I don't feel depressed, I just refuse to deny my child's (albeit brief) physical existence.

Grief and the right to Grieve

> *Some say you are too painful to remember, I*
> *say you are too precious to forget*
>
> – Author Unknown

Grief generally follows a pattern of stages, although it is perfectly normal for us to skip a stage or to return to one already visited, and this can happen again and again. I do not believe, for one moment, that the passage through bereavement fits neatly into perfect little boxes. In my experience, it is messy, chaotic and completely disordered.

Following the death of my mother, I frequently wondered if I might be going crazy. Discovering that there was a well-recognised route through my turmoil, helped me to see that everything I was encountering was perfectly natural. The following are the six main areas:

Shock

Denial/Bargaining

Anger

Guilt

Depression

Acceptance

Usually, we first feel a sense of complete *shock*, and then of numbness, as the news sinks in and a surreal feeling often kicks in, causing us to feel as if we are in a dreamlike state. This is very common. I know that when my mother first passed on, the news was permanently on my mind, but there were rare, fleeting moments of normality and then I'd suddenly be catapulted straight back into the abyss of the cold hard truth once more. I wondered if my life would ever be the same again while asking if this might be some awful nightmare that I would soon awaken from. After all, how could my life have been turned so completely on its head in such a brief period of time?

We may then enter a phase of *denial* as we try to protect ourselves from the loss. Imagining that our loved one is still somehow alive, or that what we are experiencing isn't real. Perhaps we might also begin to tell ourselves that there has been some enormous mistake, that this couldn't possibly be correct.

Bargaining for the life of our lost loved one can often occur. We may reach out to family and friends or to a higher power, pleading to have them back and promising to change certain aspects of our behaviour in return.

Being separated by distance from my mother, who was living in the UK at the time, I learned of her passing via a phone call from my sister. I can recall the date and time very clearly. I had just arrived home after collecting my youngest daughters from school one Friday afternoon New Zealand time. I noticed that the message button on the answerphone was flashing and without a second thought, pressed it and began to listen to the somewhat strained voice of my sister. She simply asked me to call her back – nothing more nothing less, but I knew in an instant exactly what she needed to say. Her tone was dull and slow, and it was four thirty in the morning, UK time.

There could only be one reason for her making contact at this hour. I can recall a cold chill spreading through me and as I stood rooted to the spot, staring out through the kitchen window, the word 'No!' repeated silently over and over again inside my head. After a few minutes, I clumsily reached for the phone and very tentatively pressed the call back button. I was extremely relieved to reach my sister's answerphone.

Ending the call, I began telling myself that everything was fine. I must have got it all wrong and busied myself by making my girls their after school snacks and embarking on vast amounts of housework and menial tasks - anything that I could find to occupy my mind and to avoid facing the reality of the situation. While I had no news of my mother, there was no need to worry I reassured myself.

Later that night, however, I finally managed to get through to my sister and my worst fears were confirmed. I could no longer hide from the truth, and there was now absolutely no chance of escaping from the devastating intoxicating pain that tore through every fibre of my being.

Next, we may feel *angry* and frustrated at the situation or with ourselves or our partners/family/medical staff, asking how this could have possibly happened! I feel that child loss is without a doubt certainly guaranteed to provoke such emotions. Of course, we sadly accept that a very sick adult or very elderly person will inevitably pass at some stage but losing a baby or a child, especially without warning or preparation, has to be the most anger rousing and intensely frustrating experience imaginable. It would be unnatural not to feel this way, and I think that great understanding is required in order to allow a grieving parent to vent as much as he or she needs to. It is vital that they should be allowed to do so without judgment and in their own time and way.

Every grieving parent has the right to express anger, and it is far better to release it than to withhold it where it could fester and cause issues. In time the anger will subside and other emotions will move in to join and eventually to replace it.

We may also start to feel *guilty* that we couldn't save our little angel, or loved one. It is crucial to know that this was *not* our fault. We did absolutely nothing wrong. If we find ourselves getting stuck at this stage, or being unable to cope with feelings of *depression*, it is a good idea to seek help from a professional such as a trained counsellor. It isn't a bad thing to accept that we may need a little help, in fact reaching out is a very brave thing to do.

Often family and friends, however well meaning, aren't really equipped to help in the way that an empathic counsellor or professional can. I would also really encourage partners to seek help too as often fathers feel that they need to remain staunch and stoic to be supportive when in reality they need to have an outlet for their grief as well. Showing their partner that they are feeling deeply affected and vulnerable can lead to a very helpful healing process for both.

A newly bereaved mother can feel completely isolated in her grief and while her partner may think that he is doing the right thing by providing a firm shoulder to cry on, what a woman really wants is to feel that she is not alone in her despair. Be open, be honest and allow each and every raw feeling to be expressed, warts and all. Your partner will thank you for it, and in some cases, it might even save your relationship.

I have included some useful telephone helpline numbers, at the back of this book, for anybody who feels the need to reach out immediately, and I would urge any person struggling with feelings of depression or anxiety to call one of the local helplines listed. If your local area support line does not appear, an online search should reveal those closest to you.

Eventually, and it may take a very long time to get to this point, we move through the pain and sorrow to a place of *acceptance*. Of course this doesn't mean that we are then 'fixed' or that we may not still have good and bad days. Due dates and anniversaries are of course especially likely to stir up a huge array of emotions.

I would like to reiterate once again that I don't believe a person should be expected to move on or to get over the loss of a baby, child or loved one ever. It has been said that grief is love with nowhere to go, and for me, this sums it up beautifully. We loved our babies from the very moment we knew of their existence, and there is no way that we can turn off such a powerful, all-consuming emotion and why should we?

Acceptance does not in any way mean that we are saying "I lost a baby but it's alright I have accepted this now." It is rather a reaching of the point at which we can say "I lost a baby and this will never be alright, but I am learning to live through my loss." Spiritually, of course, our little ones never left and continue to watch over us always. This new place of acceptance does not in any way mean that we are choosing to move on or that we are leaving our angels and loved ones behind. I see it as more of a stepping forward with our loved ones right beside us, just in the spiritual, rather than in the physical form.

Honouring our child's memory.

There are many ways that we can keep the memory of our little one alive, these might include:

Lighting a candle on baby's due date or anniversary, or on any occasion for that matter.

Releasing a balloon/balloons in his honour or placing flowers on the grave or in your home.

Meeting up with supportive family, friends or members of a baby loss support group and sharing your child's name and your experience.

Naming a rose after your child, via one of the online registries. There are also several star naming sites available, including one which is free.

Spending time in a beautiful place or creating a special area at home or in the garden in remembrance of your little one where you can sit and talk to him.

Making a memory box with treasured items inside, for example, a scan photograph, teddy bear, etc. Because I have no personal memento to remember my son by, I bought a glass butterfly ornament, and a butterfly themed candle holder in his honour.

Every Christmas, I donate a toy for a little boy, to one of the local charities here in Auckland, in memory of my son.

I'm sure that you will have many wonderful ideas of your own also.

Chapter Two

STRUGGLING ON THROUGH OUR PAIN

Do not stand at my grave and weep – Mary E Frye
Do not stand at my grave and weep
I am not there, I do not sleep.
I am a thousand winds that blow.
I am the diamond glints on snow.
I am the sunlight on ripened grain.
I am the gentle autumn rain.
Do not stand at my grave and cry;
I am not there I did not die.

These lines, taken from Mary Elizabeth Frye's beautiful poem, resonate with me so very deeply, and I asked for it to be read at my mother's funeral. We will all have our own interpretation of the poem's meaning, but for me, it epitomises my absolute belief that when we die, we don't just cease to be, but instead, continue on, our spirit omnipresent always.

After my mother had passed, I spent many hours reading through poems about bereavement. Some were heavy and dark and left me feeling even more lost and depressed, while others like the one shared, filled my broken heart with love and hope. On balance, I found the experience uplifting and frantically grabbed the all-enveloping prose with both hands. I hung on to each line that described and captured the deepest of emotions that I was enduring - both positive and negative. As dramatic as it may sound, the sentiments of these poets became like a lifeline to me. It was simply so tremendously consoling to learn that I wasn't alone in my grief and to see that others had been exactly where I was and had felt exactly how I was feeling.

Reading stories written by those who are also finding their way through the grief process, or by those who have been grieving for some time and are further on in their journey than ourselves, can be another incredibly valuable thing to do. I would definitely recommend seeking out compositions that connect with your own thoughts and feelings. I read several personal accounts that were written by people in a very similar situation to mine and am very grateful for their existence.

Alternatively (or perhaps you might like to do both) writing is also a wonderful way of releasing pent up emotion and is a very freeing experience in my opinion.

I am not talking about writing a best seller here, although you are most welcome to do so of course if you would like. The type of writing I am suggesting might consist of journaling your daily thoughts and experiences. Perhaps you'd like to write a letter to your child or loved one in spirit, or maybe even create an imagined meeting with them, and share a message of love.

If an older child or adult has passed, you could note down their responses, as if they were still with you. Perhaps you might feel like attempting to write a poem, a song or an entirely different project. There is something incredibly empowering about putting pen to paper, and I encourage you to try it. It doesn't have to make sense, it doesn't have to rhyme or even to flow particularly well. Nobody has to see your work unless you want to share it with others.

After the loss of my mother, once the initial numbness had worn off, I began writing a few sentences a day, and each one was pushed and pulled into shape by the powerful emotions I was dealing with at that time. The shock, the frustration and anger, along with the denial, guilt, and of course the deep, all-consuming sadness and longing to have just one last chat with my beautiful mum, friend and confidante.

As the weeks became months and then years, the theme of my sentences changed into fond memories and recollections of happier times. I began writing to my mum as if she were still here and said some things that I hadn't had the opportunity to say when she was alive. I found it hugely healing to unload these thoughts, and it made for compelling reading, especially as time passed by. Looking back over my scribbled notes, and delving between the numerous spelling mistakes and poor grammar, my words revealed a surprising amount of growth and a new level of insight that I'd gained along the way.

Learning to speak our truth

There is no greater agony than bearing an untold story inside you

- Maya Angelou

Most people seem to be accepting when a bereaved person expresses their grief immediately after a loss, but then get very uncomfortable when the process is prolonged, or worse still, revisited, sometime after the event. It is as if there is an unspoken time limit during which it is completely acceptable for a grieving individual to struggle, to fall to pieces and to find themselves in the all-encompassing depths of despair and desolation. Once the allotted time period has been deemed complete by those watching from the sidelines, it would appear that the time for empathy and support has passed its expiry date. An expectation of 'getting on with it' and pushing all thoughts and emotions connected to the loss swiftly aside, replaces the former.

At this point, I would recommend engaging with a like-minded person, support group or practitioner to avoid feeling alone and to continue with your journey in a supportive environment. There is nothing worse than having to suppress your emotions or thoughts because nobody seems interested in what you have to say, I have experienced this first-hand and with many different people and it is exasperating beyond belief!

As a teenager, I was frequently made to feel that my words were insignificant and that what I had to say was not worth listening to. Whenever I voiced an opinion, I was shouted down or ridiculed. Rather than allowing my speech to flow freely like a gentle stream meandering through the countryside, my thoughts and suggestions were forced rapidly downwards, way below sea level, then suffocated into oblivion!

Although much time has passed since my teenage years, I have recently been thrown right back into those painful experiences once again because I have dared to speak about my loss, and worse still, about my spiritual encounters. I have been met with complete silence and disbelief or with responses ranging from an awkward glance to the downright aggravated! Each time I spoke, every time I dared to broach the subject I could instantly sense the walls going up and that all too familiar 'here she goes again' mentality coming to the fore.

At first, I continued awkwardly on, opening up and sharing my story in the hope that the disinterested listener might soon become enlightened, might finally get it, but it seldom happened. I was left feeling embarrassed, frustrated and deeply hurt. Why couldn't they see things from my point of view? I felt that nobody cared and that they remained aloof because to understand or to empathise would be to give me unnecessary attention which in turn would enable me to continue feeling this way. The irony of the situation is of course that, had I been afforded a non-judgmental listening ear in the first place, my need to re-visit the topic, again and again, would have become superfluous.

Eventually, I learnt to be choosy and to discuss things with only like-minded people of whom there were few, but once discovered these amazing confidantes became a source of unbelievable support and comfort to me. One such person who embodies the role of an incredible earth angel perfectly, Juelle, continues to aid me. This gem of a light worker allows me to express myself comprehensively without interruption or judgement. Every bereaved parent deserves a Juelle!

I am so grateful to have her support and guidance with me on this crazy journey called life. My darling son obviously agrees with me too as he and Juelle have built up an endearing rapport. The two have had numerous conversations while I've been relaxing on the healing table, which I find tremendously amusing.

On one occasion, I felt unyielding chills spreading throughout my body, and was shocked to discover that my teeth were chattering uncontrollably, despite being in a hot room with a blanket covering me. Once the healing had been completed, Juelle told me that she had been chatting with my son, who was with us throughout the entire session.

This was such a glorious piece of news, not only because I had physically felt his presence and so incredibly intensely at that, but because of the relaxed way in which the information was shared. It was said as if Juelle had been having a nice chat with a living relative I'd just happened to take into the room with me. The entire experience left me in absolutely no doubt that our loved ones really are so incredibly close to us and that they always have been.

Chapter Three

THE DIFFERENT TYPES OF GRIEF

*It is both a blessing and a curse to feel
everything so very deeply*

– David Jones

Before studying the psychological realm, I was rather surprised to discover that there is more than one type of grief and that professionals have specific labels for each type in question. Applying labels can often be seen as a negative action, and is something that I am usually uncomfortable doing. However, I feel that when it comes to grief, it can be incredibly reassuring to know that our experience has also been encountered by others before us, and alongside us, thus strengthening the feeling that we are not alone. If a particular type of grief has been discovered and noted, then it is not something out of the ordinary.

The types of grief are:

1. *Normal Grief*

I must admit, that when I first heard about this one, I was wondering if somebody had perhaps tried to interject some humour into an otherwise very serious topic. What on earth is normal about grieving for goodness sake?! Reading further, I discovered that this type of grief contains all the elements that a person naturally moves through, including the shock, denial, anger, sadness, guilt, numb, helplessness stages and every other emotion in between. What apparently makes it normal is one's ability to move through all of the above in a gradual manner while still feeling able to continue with life, as the symptoms lessen over a period of time, and the loss is accepted.

In other words, a person who has not remained stuck in the shock or denial phases of grief, which would, of course, warrant specifically targeted support and understanding.

2. *Anticipatory Grief*

This type of grief occurs when we begin to acknowledge that a loved one's journey on earth is heading towards its conclusion. This may be due to various factors, for example, an elderly relative declining physically or mentally, perhaps due to suffering from a debilitating disease or dementia or after having a stroke. We look at our loved one and see the frailty, we witness the slow downhill transition and are coldly confronted with the fact that the inevitable is coming, maybe not this month or even this year, but coming all the same.

We begin to grieve for what was and is and will never be again. Coping with anticipatory grief can be extremely stressful.

Once our loved one has passed on, there is often a sense of relief, particularly if they were suffering or we have been tested to our limit, caring and worrying frantically for them. This feeling of consolation can cause a person to feel guilty, but it is entirely reasonable and a very natural reaction to an event that has been long anticipated.

Experiencing relief does not mean that we love the person any less, it arises solely because we have been through an overwhelming ordeal. Knowing that our loved one is no longer suffering and in pain will, of course, bring feelings of relief, and they are perfectly natural.

3. *Delayed Grief*

Delayed grief is simply grief that has been delayed for a variety of reasons. For example, a loved one passes during a tremendously busy period of our life, or the death was so traumatic that we suppress thoughts and feelings and tell ourselves that mourning will have to wait. We carry on, but the grief hits us some time later, possibly even years after the event, when something triggers us completely out of the blue and all of those 'normal' grief responses reveal themselves.

I experienced this type of grief with the loss of my son, and what made it even harder to deal with was the extraordinary circumstances in which it arose. "How can you grieve for somebody you didn't even know, and who died so long ago?" I was asked on more than one occasion.

Many were unable to comprehend why such feelings should be engulfing me after a prolonged period of time. I was also told that I had no right to grieve which left me feeling completely lost and my emotions even more displaced. To say that I struggled with the situation is a massive understatement! Thankfully I sought help from a health professional who enabled me to process my experience in a calm and understanding environment.

4. *Complicated Grief*

The criteria here involves grief that becomes severe in its longevity, is debilitating and impairs our ability to carry out everyday activities. Obviously, the symptoms of grief are going to be prominent for some time, but complicated grief goes deeper. It can cause us to exhibit more self-destructive patterns and reckless behaviour such as alcoholism, drug dependence, promiscuity and self-harm, for example. Feelings of helplessness, low self-esteem, depression, insomnia and anxiety can be all encompassing too.

If you recognise these symptoms in yourself, or in a friend or family member, please seek help. There is nothing worse than suffering in silence, and there are many wonderful professionals out there who would be only too willing to assist you with your healing. It may take a little time to find one who instantly clicks with you so don't be deterred if you aren't immediately enamoured with the first person you speak with. A referral by a GP or through word of mouth from friends or family is often a good place to start.

I don't think it was by accident that I found myself being supported through my healing journey by two health professionals who had also each lost a son. This information only came to light once I had shared my story, but it created an instant bond between us and encouraged me to unburden myself in a safe place where I felt instantly understood.

5. *Disenfranchised Grief*

What on earth is this all about you may ask? I was equally surprised when a counsellor suggested that I was suffering from this kind of grief. Disenfranchised means to deprive a person of a right or privilege, and in this context means that society regards certain types of loss as less important or not so worthy of grief. Those of us falling into this category are made to feel that our loss doesn't matter and, as a result, we are given less support, and it is not easily acknowledged by many. Of course, miscarriage and stillbirth are two prime examples, and it is annoying beyond belief that the loss of a baby should be placed in this category!

The death of an ex-partner a close friend, co-worker, in-law or pet can also be regarded as less significant. These relationships fall under the disenfranchised grief umbrella. Other examples of incidences in which we may not feel able to express our grief publicly include those where a loved one's passing is accompanied by stigma, such as in the case of an accidental drug overdose or suicide.

As we parents with angels know, society is very quick to pass judgement on the length and depth of time that we are 'allowed' to mourn our little ones. I hope that, in time, this type of grief becomes obsolete because society has had a complete re-think and has come to realise that *every* kind of grief is valid. E*very* loss deserves to be acknowledged and not just disregarded as less important than another.

Sadly, I fear that this may be a long time coming, but in the meantime, we can spread awareness and support for all who find themselves in our situation. We can honour our angels with like-minded people and express our grief exactly as and when we please!

6. *Chronic Grief*

When Chronic Grief is experienced, strong, overwhelming feelings of sadness and hopelessness regarding the loss take over, and we feel unable to cope or to move through the grief process. This type of grief can lead to severe depression and requires understanding and support in order to help an individual to make progress through the experience.

7. *Cumulative Grief*

As the name suggests, Cumulative grief is like the snowball effect, and it occurs when we encounter one loss after another in a short period of time and don't have a chance to recover from the first loss before the second takes place. This type of grief can also occur when a past loss is not fully processed and can be triggered by a second more recent one. Grieving for each individual loss is important.

8. *Collective Grief*

This type of grief is felt by a group of people, for example, a community or neighbourhood experiencing a natural disaster, a nation experiencing war or the death of a public person such as a musician or television personality.

A recent example of this occurred at the end of 2016 when the famous singer/songwriter George Michael passed on. Social media was flooded with messages of condolence, and complete strangers bared their innermost feelings and thoughts. There was a tremendous outpouring of grief as fans revealed their shock and disbelief and posted their favourite photographs of George and shared hit songs made famous by the celebrity.

9. *Abbreviated Grief*

Abbreviated Grief is a short-lived response to a loss. This may happen for several reasons, perhaps we were not very close to the person, or we had accepted that they were going to pass and had prepared for the inevitable in advance. Alternatively, the grieving process may have been shortened by something or somebody filling a void in our life.

10. *Masked Grief*

A person suffering from this type of grief may develop negative symptoms or dysfunctional behaviours which are completely out of character. They are unable to recognise that these symptoms are related to their loss.

11. *Distorted Grief*

The grief experience can be distorted by some individuals, who grossly exaggerate normal grief reactions such as anger or guilt. Noticeable changes in behaviour, which is usually reckless, are evident and they express hostility towards themselves or others.

12. *Absent Grief*

This happens when an individual shows no sign of grieving, perhaps due to shock or denial. Sometimes a person grieves in private and then manages to hold it together in public, in this case, there is not a problem. If a person is not grieving in private either, then this is a concern, especially if the denial continues for an extended period of time. Sudden and traumatic deaths often provoke this type of grief.

If you find yourself identifying with one or more of the types of grief mentioned, please know that you are not alone. I would really encourage you to reach out for help, and if you can relate to any of the more severe forms of grief described, it is imperative that you do so. It takes a great deal of courage to acknowledge that something isn't quite right and taking the step to confide in somebody, whether it be a friend, family member, counsellor or other professional, reveals a tremendous amount of strength.

PART TWO

CONNECTING WITH OUR HIGHER SELF

Chapter Four

OUT OF THE MOUTHS OF BABES

Heaven lies about us in our infancy

– William Wordsworth

As a young child, dolls and teddy bears were my constant companions. I relished caring for them and spent many joyful hours playing happy families. Looking back, my maternal instinct seems to have kicked in very early on.

Apparently, at around the age of three, I also acquired an invisible friend who would tag along with us on family outings, join us for dinner and take part in all household activities. I have no recollection of this but am told that my playmate was a large part of my life for at least a year. In hindsight, I do now wonder if my visiting chum may have in fact been a spirit.

In recent years, I have come to understand that many children, before the age of five or six, while still innocent and unaware of the norms, expectations and perceived beliefs of the adult world, encounter invisible friends. Once school life begins and routine and order become a way of life, somewhere along the line, logic steps in and little ones realise that perhaps these experiences are best kept to themselves. A kind of switching off takes place, and further experiences are blocked or discounted.

I have heard numerous recounts from parents who have reported watching their children staring, in a highly unusually engrossed way, at something (or somebody) for a prolonged period of time. These parents could not explain the intense focus displayed by their little ones and stood by feeling utterly spooked!

One parent also caught her child talking animatedly and convincingly to some concealed entity who seemed to be in quite close proximity to the little girl, despite remaining entirely undetectable to her extremely anxious mother.

While watching a television programme covering the topic, many years ago, I was completely engrossed to hear about one very perceptive little boy, who caught the attention of his teachers while playing outside in the garden at his nursery school. The building in which he spent three mornings a week was located slap bang in the middle of two cemeteries.

One morning, a member of staff spotted the child standing rigidly, eyes fixed, at an area towards one corner of the plot. The little boy's stance and stillness were so out of character that the teacher quickly called to a colleague and the two watched with surprise and immediately agreed that there was something completely unexplainable occurring!

In a separate incident, this same little chap pointed to his then three-month pregnant mother's stomach and in a very matter of fact way, announced that "Baby gone." Sadly, his mother miscarried a short time after the prediction. Thankfully a more joyful foretelling was made a year later when, once again, cuddling up to Mum's growing baby bump, it was suggested that he was going to have a baby sister. The ultrasound scan, a couple of weeks later, confirmed the little three-year-olds prediction.

A second recount recalled a grandparent who was sitting with her three-year-old granddaughter one afternoon. Completely out of the blue, the little girl announced that she had chosen her Mummy and Daddy "When I was looking down from the top of the trees." When asked why she had chosen this particular set of parents, the wise little soul explained that she knew they wanted a little baby to love and care for and also went on to reveal that she also wanted to make sure that her Nanny (who had been living alone for quite some time) wasn't lonely.

Out of the mouths of babes is an expression you may have heard of before. I think it fits in here rather nicely and I'm very much looking forward to discovering further tales and words of wisdom that have been shared by spiritually sensitive little ones.

In his book 'Memories of Heaven,' Dr Wayne Dyer interviewed hundreds of parents who expressed that their children had also 'taken part' in one or more spiritual experiences. Many relayed conversations in which a little one had accurately described a deceased family member, never before seen or heard of by the child. I have also read accounts of small children remembering past lives that they lived as adults. In some instances, children were able to provide precise details concerning their family members, occupations and even the circumstances surrounding their deaths.

Dr Dyer explained how many of the children he interviewed, also spoke of choosing their parents from a group of prospective parents-to-be before conception had even taken place

I personally find the suggestion that we parents were pre-selected by our children an incredibly moving one, and I hope that you can take some comfort from knowing that your little angel chose you because of all the wonderful qualities that you possess. No matter how brief their earthly life, of all the potential parents in the world, your precious little one chose you.

Chapter Five

ALL THAT I KNOW

Our birth is but a sleep and a forgetting

– William Wordsworth

At the grand old age of ten years and four months, I declared quite categorically that I was going to be a mum, and also an actress or a teacher when I grew up. My friend Lisa who, at almost twelve years old, and therefore extremely wise and knowledgeable in my eyes, declared that she would be a vet, and maybe a mum too.

I can remember feeling completely shocked by her response, not because I thought that she'd selected poorly but because I couldn't believe that becoming a mother was only a possibility for her. Those maternal instincts of mine had certainly not faded with time!.

"How many children do you want?" Lisa asked

"Not sure, but a few" I replied. "Maybe four?"

"Really? That's a lot of children."

"Maybe three then and one of them is going to be a boy" I continued.

"Right, but how do you know one will be a boy?"

I can, to this day, recall so clearly, sitting on my bed gazing across the room toward the window, desperately searching for words that could accurately convey the absolute certainty that I felt. There were no words, how could I ever hope to describe such an undeniable *knowing?* I had never questioned the why and how before now, there was no need to, I just knew! Eventually, I found myself responding with three very unimpressive words which nevertheless spoke from the heart...

"I just *do.*"

Later that night, I sat chatting with Mum about her relatives. Sadly, I never had the chance to meet either of my maternal grandparents because they both passed on before I was born. I knew that my grandfather's parents had lived in and around London all of their lives, but Mum was quite reluctant to discuss her mother's side of the family. I hadn't liked to push things in the past because I knew that my grandmother had passed at just 46 years of age, leaving a husband and five children.

The youngsters were all wrenched away from the family home and farmed out to various children's homes and relatives, when my grandfather, unable to cope, began drinking heavily. I didn't want to upset my mother, but I was so eager to learn more about my grandmother and her parents who were born and lived in Belfast, Northern Ireland.

I felt quite a pull to the Emerald Isle and longed for more information. Unfortunately, the facts given were extremely minimal, to say the least!

I have since researched this side of my family quite extensively and have discovered that my great-grandfather, Alex, worked as a labourer, at the docks where the famous ship RMS Titanic was built. This snippet of information was to prove extremely imperative in one of my readings, which I shall reveal later in the book.

All things Irish had certainly captured my imagination and I began looking at Gaelic names. There were some beautiful and many almost unpronounceable ones. It took me a while to ascertain the correct pronunciation of such lovely names as Siobhan and Oisin! One name, in particular, stood out amongst the rest and instantly captured my heart. I especially loved the English spelling of it – *Kieran*, I recited the name silently in my head, several times, and then spoke it out loud "Kieran" It resonated deeply within for some reason and I knew, at that moment, that I had been presented with my son's name.

Teenage Dreams

As I reached my teenage years, all thoughts of becoming a mother were replaced by crucial considerations such as which one of my bedroom walls' my favourite pop stars Simon Le Bon from the group *Duran Duran* and Tony Hadley, lead singer of the band *Spandau Ballet*'s posters should be stuck to. Fashion and makeup became vital talking points, and Saturdays were spent scouring the shops of Enfield, my hometown, in search of the latest accessories. Party planning and researching the best discos were hot topics for my friends and I.

At the age of sixteen, I became an aunt to my sister Sue's beautiful daughter Claire. Because Sue was still living in the family home for the first months of her little one's life, I experienced first-hand, the joys and difficulties of becoming a mother. I shared a bedroom with my sister, so I also had a fast initiation into every new mother's world of sleep deprivation! Amazingly, despite living in very cramped noisy conditions, I never once felt deterred from having a baby of my own, not even after attempting my first ever nappy change, which my sister and I still laugh about to this day. I can clearly remember adorning myself with a pair of woolly gloves and a scarf, which I tied tightly around my face, to form a mask as if preparing for some deadly procedure, and cautiously stating "I'm going in!"

Fortunately, after my initial encounter of the nappy kind, subsequent changes were performed with much less fuss, much to baby Claire's relief I'm sure. I loved being an aunt and taking my niece on outings to the local park, and although it was very cramped in our tiny terraced house of six, it was a truly sombre day when my sister moved out. On the plus side, however, my sleep pattern improved immensely!

A few months before my seventeenth birthday, having

finished my exams and reaching the end of school life, I secured my first ever job working as a receptionist for a local company. I felt quite pleased with myself for obtaining a full-time job at just sixteen and as I was unsure of exactly which career path to follow at that point, gaining employment and earning some money while I decided, seemed to be the best option.

My weekly wage packet opened up a whole new world for a once penniless school girl, and it was a good feeling being able to help Mum and Dad a little as money was always short at home.

I can recall spending my very first wage packet on cassette tapes and vinyl records at the music shop HMV, make up at Woolworths department store and on clothes at the popular teenage girl's shop - Top Shop. I can also remember feeling very grown up when a new nightclub called The Pink Elephant opened in nearby Southgate. My friends and I were at the front of the queue on opening night, waiting to have ID photographs taken. It would have been December 1983 at this point, because Michael Jackson's famous 'Thriller' video had just been produced and was presented in its full glory across the club's mega projection screen. It was a great night and one that my friends, Jenny, Debbie, Annette and I talked about for weeks afterwards.

With my eighteenth birthday just around the corner, I decided to pop into town, in search of an outfit to wear for the girl's night out I had planned with a few friends. Excitedly, I approached the shopping precinct and headed for my favourite clothes shops, eagerly hoping to find a great dress or a new top and jeans.

As I walked determinedly on, my attention was abruptly caught by a window dresser, who was adding the final touches to a display of baby clothing in the main window of the baby shop Mothercare. I paused for a moment to admire the cute little outfits, then found myself entering the shop and heading for the newborn section.

Bearing in mind that I was seventeen and single at the time, feeling this drawn to look at baby equipment and clothing, was certainly unusual - to say the least! The most surprising thing of all was that it didn't feel odd at the time, though. It felt entirely natural that I should pick out an outfit for my future baby, and absolutely right that I should choose from the blue department.

I selected a lovely little navy and white sailor style romper suit with matching white socks and pictured my little boy looking so cute and scrumptious wearing it. Once home, I placed the clothes inside a suitcase which I then closed tight and pushed as far under my bed as possible. I knew that my parents and younger brother might be somewhat alarmed to discover my hidden treasure and might go so far as to question my sanity if they were to discover it.

Pondering further and imagining their shocked faces, I reached beneath the bed once more, retrieved the case and buried the outfit, with the tenacity of a dog hiding a beloved bone that no predator would ever uncover, beneath a pile of old school books and papers. Feeling satisfied that my secret stash was now perfectly safe, I once again concealed the case and went back to organising my birthday celebrations.

Shortly after my eighteenth birthday, I decided to hand in my notice at work and embarked on a Nursery Nursing course at nearby Barnet College. I loved children and knew that I would enjoy a career in this field, there was also the option to go on to teacher training, which really appealed to me. I cherished working with the children in nursery and infant schools and was then offered a job as a children's nanny, by a fabulous family, which I happily accepted. I had sole charge of a lovely little three-month-old boy and subsequently his younger sister. I am still in touch with them after all of these years and have very fond memories of caring for my two charges, Joe and Katie.

I met my best friend and soul mate, Mark, two years later, and in 1991 we married and have been together ever since.

PART THREE

EARTHLY CHALLENGES

Chapter Six

MY JOURNEY TOWARDS MOTHERHOOD

Sometimes the smallest things take up the most room in your heart

– A.A Milne

Although I would have happily jumped into starting a family immediately after we were married, Mark, ever the practical one, asked if I would work for one more year to boost our savings. I reluctantly agreed and counted down the months weeks and days until finally, the year was up!

I imagined that getting pregnant would be a piece of cake, something that would happen easily and quickly, but after almost a year of trying to conceive, there was still no baby. I was convinced that something must be terribly wrong, and we agreed that if nothing had changed in the next few months, then we'd go for tests. In hindsight, I realise that for some poor couples, a year is absolutely nothing, but at the time, a year seemed like a lifetime to me, and I was seriously doubting if I would ever get to live my dream of becoming a mother.

My poor husband must have been at the end of his tether, watching me fall apart each month at the realisation that there was no pregnancy. I had felt so sure, on a couple of occasions, that there had been too (and once years earlier,) but had fought the desire to carry out a pregnancy test in case I jinxed things!

Looking back the signs were there, but I still feel terribly guilty when I hear of other women's excruciatingly painful experiences of miscarriage. After researching the subject, I discovered that the rate of miscarriage in the early stages of pregnancy is incredibly high and if no pregnancy test had been carried out, many more women who were unaware that they were pregnant could be added, making the figures even higher. I considered the dilemma before me.

I feel incredibly thankful that I was spared the devastating pain and heartbreak of knowing that my baby had passed, yet there is also a huge part of me that wishes I'd known that my child had existed, that he had lived within me no matter how briefly. There must be thousands of women who are unaware that they have little angels around them and whose short lives have never been acknowledged and I find this concept incredibly sad. Had my son not made his presence known in later years, I would have also been one of the statistics.

After twelve and a half long months, a positive pregnancy

test revealed that we were finally going to be parents. To say that I was over the moon is a gigantic understatement! I was absolutely ecstatic, and alongside my wedding day, this was without a doubt, the best day of my life thus far.

Eight months later, our beautiful daughter entered the world and created a new best day of my life. She greeted us completely alert, as calm as a cucumber, taking in her surroundings and then gazing knowingly at the two of us as if to say "Hello, I'm back again." This little cherub really did seem like a wise old soul who had been here before, and has grown into an amazing compassionate young woman who I am so incredibly proud to call my daughter.

In 1995, our family of three became four, as we welcomed a second daughter into the clan. Our gorgeous bundle of fun seemed rather annoyed at joining her earthly family, and we joke about her having second thoughts on arrival. Her loyalty, determination and loving nature have served her well in life, and she is now a wonderful young woman and a blessing, who makes me very proud.

Our third daughter was extremely reluctant to make an entrance and to this day, remains a very easy going, kind and thoughtful young lady and a champion for the underdog. I am very proud of her and am so delighted that she chose to join the craziness of our family. She is an absolute blessing, who I would choose to have in my corner without hesitation.

And baby makes six! Our family was completed by a fourth sugar and spice and all things nice, when in 2002, I gave birth to a fourth daughter who arrived extremely expeditiously, just five minutes after entering the delivery room! She remains an entirely active blessing and has a deep passion for animals and animal welfare. I feel so proud watching as she devotes her time to nursing sick animals come rain or shine, without complaint.

Raising four children has not been without its challenges, but I love motherhood and caring for my girls. Between the school, drop offs and pickups, after school and weekend activities, there was never a dull moment when they were young, but I wouldn't change one single day of it. Well, actually, I might trade in some of the sleepless nights! Life was very full on but great fun, and I had little time to question the non-appearance of my bundle of blue or to consider just how wrong I had been despite my irrefutable knowing.

People would pass comments such as "Four girls, Wow!" and I would respond with a nod and a "Yes, my poor husband will be completely henpecked!" Worse was the inevitable "Four girls, I expect you were hoping for a boy?." I would feign a smile and act as if this was the first rather than the one-hundredth time I'd heard this remark, longing to respond with "Actually, I was hoping for four healthy children, and I am incredibly thankful for each of them, is that a problem?" but instead, saying nothing. I can remember on one occasion, the mother of one of my eldest daughter's friends asking if I'd like to hold her baby boy "To see what it feels like" People can be so tactless!

Chapter Seven

LIFE TAKES A DIFFERENT PATH

*Sometimes your only available transportation
is a leap of faith*

– Margaret Shepard

In April 2005, I overheard my husband, Mark, chatting on the phone with an old school friend, Paul, who had recently obtained employment in Auckland, New Zealand, and had moved his family across the world for a two-year placement. My husband was listening in awe as Paul described the beauty and vast opportunities that the country had to offer. It was obvious that Paul was encouraging us to consider the move also, and I was a little taken aback to hear the following words of dismissal flowing from Mark's mouth…"Oh, Lorraine would never leave her family."

Well, I will let you into a little secret, I can be very stubborn, and being told that I won't do something often has the opposite effect on me! Later that evening, I asked Mark why he had presumed my answer without actually discussing things with me, and found myself making one of the biggest decisions of my life. I agreed to up sticks, leave my family and friends in London and move across to the other side of the world, just about as far away as I could possibly imagine, for a two-year trial period. I am atrocious at making small decisions, but it seems that humongous, life changing ones are a piece of cake!

My supportive Mum agreed to take care of the girls for a fortnight while Mark and I went on a whirlwind tour of Auckland and various other parts of the North Island of NZ, to ensure that we would be making the right decision by uprooting our children and changing their lives forever.

We returned to England at the end of May, armed with photographs, souvenirs and video clips to show the girls, alongside multiple job offers for Mark, and on August 21st, after the most intolerable farewell to family and friends, boarded the first of our two flights to Auckland.

If somebody had told me at that point in time just how utterly complicated and overwhelming the next couple of years would prove to be, I would have sprinted right off that plane in a flash!

Our first weeks in New Zealand were filled with excitement and discovery as we explored Auckland and visited as many of the tourist attractions that we could cram in, before settling down to the more serious task of finding a suitable permanent location to live, and choosing schools for the girls. After much to-ing and fro-ing, we eventually managed to secure a base and places at two schools. At this point, we moved from the 'holiday' phase to the real life one!

We had decided to have our furniture and worldly possessions shipped over in the hope that having familiar things around would help the girls (and us!) to feel more settled. We were extremely fortunate that Mark's new company had agreed to pay for the container, alongside our flights and initial accommodation, providing that he remained with the company for at least a year. We were very grateful, and the container departed several weeks before we left, ready to greet us no more than five or six weeks after our arrival.

Unfortunately, the ship carrying the container somehow managed to divert off course, and at one point it was unclear if we'd ever be reunited with our worldly goods again! I wasn't concerned about the big things, but all of the children's photographs, their artwork and other very sentimental and irreplaceable items were on that ship. Unsurprisingly I experienced my first real pang of homesickness at this point.

Thankfully, one week before Christmas, and almost ten weeks later than expected, we received the most wonderful news. The ship had docked, and the contents of our container were finally on their way.

Despite the initial niggles associated with moving six people away from home and all that is familiar, to the other side of the world, we settled in reasonably well. I really missed my family, we were very close, and I was in almost daily contact with them before we left, but we spoke frequently. Mum and I would chat for a few hours each week, and it definitely helped to bridge the gap a little.

We had fun getting to explore different parts of the country and experienced things that we could never have imagined had we not taken such a huge leap of faith. I recall one of the girls coming out of school, one afternoon, waving a piece of paper in front of me, and explaining that a popular children's TV programme was looking for a child to film at home, for a segment of the show. "We just have to call this number Mum!" she instructed, her little face beaming at the prospect of making her television debut. I was, of course terribly cynical. At best, I was sure that dialling the number would result in being put through to a pre-recorded voice message reciting basic instructions. I imagined we'd be asked to 'leave our details' (along with the tens of thousands of other eagerly over excited children) This would surely have been the scenario had we been calling in the UK, but this was New Zealand after all, the land of opportunity. Just ten minutes later, I was speaking with the producer and making an appointment for the film crew to visit us the following week!

Eleven months after our arrival in Auckland, we received a phone call that would drastically reinforce the vast distance between our loved ones back home and ourselves. My mother in law had been rushed to hospital for a blood transfusion, after being misinformed by her GP that she was anaemic and that taking iron tablets would be enough to improve her condition. Apparently, this was just not the case, something much more serious was occurring, and she had undergone emergency surgery to have her spleen removed, had contracted MRSA, the hospital superbug and had also been placed in an induced coma! I was stunned, and couldn't imagine what my poor husband must have been going through.

After some in depth discussion, we decided that the logistics of transporting six people 12.000 miles away would be too difficult to achieve in such a time essential situation, so, very reluctantly, I had to step back and for the first time in our then, twenty year relationship, couldn't be there for my best friend. All I could do was to pray that Mark would make it all the way home before his mother passed.

Thankfully, my mother in law was brought out of the coma just before her only surviving child arrived and was thrilled to see him. They spent a week together before Teresa left the earthly plane, and joined her daughter Angela who had passed eleven years earlier at the tender age of just twenty-five.

In July 2007, we decided that it would be good to experience a more rural lifestyle. We had lived in a town in England, and here we were living in another despite the miles and miles of green space and Bush - not to mention the abundance of fabulous beaches surrounding us. New Zealand really is a nature lover's paradise. Besides, we had promised the girls pets, and a dog and cat were at the top of the list. I quite fancied raising some little lambs or goats too. So, we bit the bullet and moved once again. This time to a rural area in the north of Auckland which is a lovely place, far enough from the city to enjoy all that the countryside has to offer, but close enough not to be out in the sticks. We didn't want the girls to feel isolated from friends and felt it important that they kept their independence.

The two youngest girls attended the local country school and enjoyed raising day-old chicks into hens, and bottle feeding rejected lambs and watching them grow. They enjoyed taking part in their first ever school agricultural day, and we were all adapting to becoming country folk reasonably well.

We didn't have much choice to be honest, as the people we bought our house from had told us that the wild sheep grazing in the paddocks were owned by our neighbour. However, when no contact had been made after some weeks, we decided to ask our new friends if they were ready to move their stock back into their own paddocks so that we could reclaim the grass for some animals of our own. I'm sure you can imagine our surprise when we were notified that the unruly, un-shorn mob belonged to us. Apparently, it had slipped the previous owners minds to mention that the house came with a free flock of sheep!

Immediately, we hit the Internet and grabbed every book that we could find at the local library, searching for as much information as we could about caring for the woolly beasts. I felt very sorry for them as it was clear that they had not been very well cared for. The following months consisted of a mass shearing, worming, drenching, applying anti-fly strike sprays, caring for hooves and offering as many food pellets as we could, to tame and prove to the sheep that we weren't the enemy.

Fortunately, we managed to convince almost every last Ewe and Ram, and not a second too soon because just a few weeks later, we were met by the incredible sight of two little lambs nestled against a very protective mum. Over the next eight weeks, we acquired a further nine little lambs. To say that we were thrown into the ways of the countryside rather quickly is a massive understatement, but it is one that we wouldn't change, and I am incredibly grateful that the sheep were so patient with us amateurs!

Chapter Eight

IT'S ALWAYS DARKEST BEFORE THE DAWN

The most painful goodbyes are the ones that
are never said and never explained

- Bilal Nasir Khan

Each New Year's Eve, no matter where I was or what I was
doing, a phone call to Mum was a must. We continued the
tradition even after I had emigrated, with the added twist of
speaking at both our NZ and UK midnights. On December
31st, 2007, Mum failed to answer my call, and I knew
immediately that something was wrong. My mother lived
alone because she and my father had divorced many years
before and there was nobody else available to take the call.

After many frantic calls to my brother and father and a
very sleepless night, we finally learned that Mum had been
rushed to hospital after a home check up with the visiting

doctor, revealed that there was so much fluid around her heart, the beats could hardly be detected!

A few days later, we received the tragic news that the cancer Mum had fought so bravely to overcome nine years earlier, had returned. Last time around, I had been there, taking my mother to some of her chemotherapy and radiotherapy appointments, collecting her after her surgery, watching and listening and generally making sure that she was ok, but this time...what use was I living so very far away? I felt incredibly frustrated and wished that I had never left England. This beautiful country that I had chosen to adopt as home, suddenly became my prison and I felt well and truly trapped!

I took my youngest two daughters back to visit Mum, and for just over three weeks, we spent some quality time together which was lovely. When the dreaded last day of our trip arrived, I was mentally preparing myself for the most intolerably painful final goodbye, but no amount of preparation could ever have been enough. I knew that it was unlikely I would ever get to see my mother again...I was right, just six months later I received the harrowing news that she had passed on.

Although we knew that this was inevitable, it still came as a huge shock. There had been many occasions in which the medical staff had warned us that Mum might not pull through the night, only for her to prove them wrong and to carry on time and time again. I had spoken with her just two days beforehand, and she had sounded great. When this brave lady finally took her last breath, nobody was prepared. There had been no warning, and no expectation and it came like a bolt out of the blue!

On discovering the news, I hid my grief from my family because I didn't want to worry them. In hindsight, I wish I'd let them in and allowed them to see how much the loss of my mother had affected me. Instead, I did what I had always done and pushed my emotions down, carrying on as if everything was okay, while all the time it felt as if I was sinking into a dark black hole. I wondered if I would ever be able to claw my way back out of it.

Because of financial and time constraints, I was unable to return home to England for my mother's funeral. If anybody had predicted that I would not be there, I would have told them not to be so ridiculous. Missing my own mother's funeral was simply out of the question. The guilt of not being present at her sending off is something that has tormented me for many years, and I am only now beginning to free myself from its vice like grip.

The possibility that there might be an afterlife, and all of the mysteries surrounding it, had never really caught my attention before Mum's passing, despite experiencing many losses in my family, including those of my grandparents, three Uncles, my sister in law and mother in law. I did have a funny encounter of the spiritual kind when pregnant with my first daughter, however.

I discovered that I was expecting on the day of my Uncle Dave's funeral. I was very close to Mum's youngest brother who passed at just 48 years of age, and a few months after his transition home, while lying in bed, sleep eluding me, my Uncle suddenly 'appeared' at the foot of my bed! Immediately, I dived beneath the duvet, my heart pounding fiercely through my chest. I feared that I might have a heart attack or suffocate, but there was no way I was venturing back outside the safety and confines of my hiding place!

Eventually, the prospect of dying became greater than my fear of seeing the ghostly figure again so I, very cautiously and very hesitantly, forced myself to peer over the top of the duvet to discover...there was nobody - or no spirit, perhaps I should say, there.

The following morning, I managed to convince myself that it must have been nothing more than my imagination, or a dream. Still, I couldn't quite shake off the feeling of it being much more than that, and I knew categorically that my eyes were wide open at the time the apparition appeared!

PART FOUR

AWAKENING

Chapter Nine

THE FRUSTRATING AND
THE FANTASTIC

All things are possible for those who believe

- Anon

About a year after my mother's passing, I began researching all things spiritual. I was extremely interested in reading books about re-incarnation, and Dr Brian Weiss, author of a variety of such books, including his most famous 'Many Lives, Many Masters' particularly intrigued me.

Around this time, I also met a couple of spiritually minded friends and one of them, Ellen, invited me to attend the local Spiritualist church with her later that week. I was very much in two minds about going, mostly because I wasn't quite sure what to expect. Curiosity eventually caught the better of me however and three evenings later, I found myself entering a small community hall in nearby Silverdale. Once inside, I headed straight for the back row of chairs and took a seat in the far corner where I could hide, but also make a quick getaway should the need arise!

The evening began with an address by the chairperson, and after a warm welcome, we were all invited to stand to sing an upbeat song from the folder located beneath our seats. I later learned that singing would raise the energetic vibration in the hall. Next, came the general notices followed by a short talk from the visiting medium, who explained how she had discovered her gift. It was fascinating, and I found myself relaxing, relieved that I had experienced no head spinning or similar terrifying occurrences!

After a second upbeat sing along, we sat and prepared to listen to messages from loved ones who had passed on. Being a newbie, I didn't hold out any hope of receiving a message, and that was completely fine. I much preferred to be an observer.

"I'd like to come to the lady with dark hair in the back row" began the medium, and I turned discreetly to view the dark haired woman behind me, only to discover that there was nobody there and that I was indeed sitting in the very back row! Gathering my thoughts as quickly as I could, I smiled nervously and wondered what on earth she was going to say to me. Perhaps Mum had popped in to let me know she was alright, or maybe my lovely Nan, Doris, or one of my Uncles were here to say "Hello" I felt my heart racing and struggled to gain my composure, but the medium continued looking directly at me.

"Your eldest child is a boy isn't he?" she asked assuredly, looking for instant validation.

"No" I replied, apologetically, "My eldest is a daughter, I don't have a son."

I felt sorry for the medium, and she looked clearly shocked and genuinely surprised. My rejection seemed to throw her off course, and she struggled to continue, taking a few minutes to process our brief interaction, before stating that she would come back to me, and moving swiftly on! Her subsequent readings seemed to be accepted very favourably by all recipients, so how had she been so misguided with me I wondered?

Despite feeling for her, I was also disappointed that she hadn't brought Mum through. My first real experience of mediumship left me feeling somewhat deflated, and I doubted that I'd ever return to the church again.

At the start of 2012, we had been living in Auckland for six and a half years. We'd had many great, and a few not so great times, but by now, everybody had settled well in Kiwi-land. Everybody that is, except for me. I was so pleased that we had chosen to give our children this fantastic opportunity, but I missed my family and friends in England desperately and wondered if I would ever consider New Zealand my home. I felt quite selfish for feeling this way and tried to hide my feelings from everybody, though my poor husband did suffer the brunt of my frustration from time to time.

In hindsight, I was probably still grieving the loss of

my mother, and I very much felt the presence of a black cloud constantly hovering above my head and also had an unshakable feeling that something was missing from my life, but what that 'something' was, I just couldn't say.

My eldest daughter is a very sensitive, empathic young woman, so it didn't come as a great surprise when she admitted to me that she had experienced a few unexplained occurrences herself. She had also recently seen a notice advertising a 'Psychic Fundraiser' that was taking place in the city and wondered if I would accompany her to it. She continued to explain that it involved a lot of mediums and clairvoyants, giving ten-minute readings for the very reasonable sum of just two dollars. We would take a seat in front of a particular reader of our choice, have the reading then move on to a seat in the queue of a second reader's table, and then a third and so on. I was unsure at first and doubted that much information could be given in such a short time frame, but my daughter was very keen, so I agreed to go along.

The venue, a large community hall, was jam-packed with people hoping to hear from loved ones and I wondered if we should just turn around and walk out. My inquisitive nature once again got the better of me, however, and a few minutes later I was sitting in a seemingly never ending queue.

Eventually, my turn transpired, and I handed the reader, Peter, my gold coin donation and listened eagerly. He was very spot on with a lot of the information brought forward, and I soon realised that he was a clairvoyant rather than a medium, that is to say, he talked about events from my past, present and a little about my future.

It was all very interesting, but I really longed for contact with my deceased loved ones. As the bell announcing the end of the ten-minute session rang, I thanked Peter for his insight and his (very kind and slightly amusing) estimation that my intuition is about 98.4% accurate and that I should always pay attention to it, and surveyed the hall looking for a second reader.

I made for a very friendly looking lady's table, but after thirty minutes decided to abandon my place in the relentless line of chairs and headed over to a wise looking woman who was giving a reading at that moment and had just one person in her queue. Looking back, I believe that spirit directed me to this second lady...

"Hello, how are you? I'm Betty" she began, and continued to relay the following information:

Betty "I can see a child, a little boy."

Me "I don't have a little boy, I have four daughters."

Betty (looking rather confused) "Right, well I would like to say that your girls are all well-adjusted and very happy in their own skins."

Me "Thank you, yes that's true."

Betty "Your eldest daughter knows exactly what she wants and goes for it! Your second daughter can be quite strong willed but has a good heart."

Me (laughing) "Yes, you have them spot on. I love them both to bits though."

Betty "Your third daughter is a very well behaved girl, though she is trying to keep up with her older sisters and she is very sensitive. Your youngest daughter wraps your husband around her little finger, but she is a real Mummy's girl. What is it with the bad headaches? That's not right, she shouldn't be suffering at her age should she?"

Me "Yes, you have described all the girls to a tee."

Side Note: I didn't respond to the comment about my daughter having headaches because she was completely trouble free at that time. However, three years later, in 2015, the comment was proven amazingly accurate, when, after six months of intense, excruciating headaches, my youngest daughter was diagnosed as suffering from Migraine with Aura.

Betty "I can see you taking up a form of study, are you thinking of doing something like counselling at all?"

Me "Yes, I have recently enrolled on a counselling course, and I start my training in a couple of months' time."

Betty "I think this is a perfect thing for you to do. Are you having some renovations done at home, I can see some tiles and tins of paint?"

Me "Yes, my husband is renovating our bathroom."

Betty "It's looking good! Don't let him overdo it, though, he is very active isn't he? He never stops! He needs to put his feet up more."

Me "Absolutely! He is always on the go. He loves to have a project to tackle at all times, and has recently run a marathon."

Betty "Do we have Mum in spirit?"

Me (excitedly) "Yes!"

Betty "She is showing me that you have her hair. She is very well and is with her school friend Rose. She also tells me that she has been moving a family picture around that you have at home."

Me "Yes I do, her mother had the same dark wavy hair, also. We looked very alike. I can't quite place Rose, at this time, but I don't know all of Mum's friends, especially going back to her childhood. The photo, Oh my goodness. Just before leaving England, we had a photograph taken of my family and my husband's family combined. Mum is standing in the centre of it. I keep it on the windowsill in my lounge, and it

71

keeps moving forward. I am the only person that dusts and would, therefore, handle it, but it seems to move every few days. I have interrogated my husband and the girls, but they all deny touching it. That's so funny!"

Betty "It's Mum's way of letting you know that she is still with you."

At this point, the bell rang signalling the end of the ten-minute session.

Chapter Ten

MY EPIPHANY

Reason is powerless in the expression of love

– Rumi

The following day, I treated myself to a gold coloured book and decided to transfer the rapidly scribbled notes from yesterday's readings, into it, word for word, exactly as the readers had delivered them. I thought it might be fun to refer to the messages from time to time. Fortunately, I have done the same with every reading I have had since that day.

Later that night, while relaxing in bed, I found myself gently processing the events of the previous day. I was so grateful to my dear Mum for coming through and knowing that she was absolutely well and happy and of course still with me, brought me a huge deal of relief and comfort. I thought about the beginning of the reading and the mention of the little boy, and wondered what on earth that was all about! It took me right back to the night spent at the

Spiritualist church, a couple of years previously, when the medium suggested that my firstborn was a son, what was it with these mediums?

I recollected a third incident in which my sister had asked me to accompany her to a reading back in Enfield, when my eldest daughter was about a year old. This experience had completely slipped my mind until now. I can't remember much of the information presented to me that evening, but one thing that I had been told seemed to have much more meaning now "I can see a little baby boy in a crib, but you know that already don't you?"

Having never visited a medium before, I didn't want to appear like a complete novice, so rather than show my ignorance I just nodded and smiled. Unsure still, I presumed that this was simply an indication of things to come in the future. How I wish now that I had asked the reader for clarification!

Just then, suddenly, and completely out of nowhere, BOOM! It hit me like a tonne of bricks, *a complete epiphany!* - The suitcase under my bed containing the baby boy outfit, (long since donated to a local charity shop), the absolute certainty that I was going to have a son all of those years ago, the inescapable feeling that something (or somebody perhaps?) was missing from my life... Could I have lost a son? Was it possible? Had I gone crazy?! Was this wishful thinking? An overactive imagination perhaps?

My mind was awash with an abundance of questions, and I scolded myself for getting quite so carried away. I tried to remain completely rational. This must be nothing more than coincidence I told myself. Of course I would have known if I had lost a baby...wouldn't I? There was obviously some completely normal explanation, I just hadn't considered it yet!

Several days later, when the niggling questions had still not abated, despite my best efforts to silence them, I knew that I was never going to resolve the uncertainty unless I dealt with it head on. I needed to have a one to one reading with a medium, and this time I vowed not to discard even the slightest mention of a little boy! The only question now, of course, was where would I find such a person? I had no recommendations to follow, and I really didn't want to draw attention to the situation, because I knew that, most of my family members and some of my friends would be incredibly cynical, to say the least.

This was such a mind-boggling, extraordinary experience, and I needed to keep it to myself, for now at least. I headed to the Internet and randomly selected a medium. The lady in question, Kate had good testimonials and looked trustworthy enough, so I took the plunge and emailed her asking when she next had availability. A few hours later I received a reply explaining that she was fully booked until Easter Sunday, which was a whole fortnight away! I accepted immediately and kept myself very busy in the interim.

The Most Precious Gift

Finally, Sunday, March 31st, 2013 came around, and I set off to meet Kate at a community hall not too far from me.

I arrived a little earlier than my appointment time and sat
in my car anxiously waiting for the door to open, signalling
my time to enter the building. As I sat there, literally not
knowing what to expect from our meeting, I offered a request
to my potential son in spirit, which felt slightly odd I must
confess. I asked the following:

"If this is real, and you are real, and not a figment of
my imagination or simply a case of wishful thinking, please
would you come through and give me a sign? Perhaps your
age or initial or something, anything, just so that I can know,
once and for all, thank you" I had just completed my plea
when the door opened, and Kate appeared, beckoning me
towards her.

After a brief introduction, we shook hands and entered
the large bare hall. The only furniture present was a table and
two chairs. I was invited to sit and to place my collection of
photographs on the table. (Kate had asked me to bring in a
small selection of photos of loved ones, which she would then
read energetically)

Firstly she invited me to write my full maiden and
married names along with the months of the year onto a piece
of paper. It seemed like a strange request at the time, but in
hindsight, I presume she wanted me to transfer some of my
energy which she would then read. Kate explained that the
information would come through like very rapid quick fire,
so I needed to be ready with my pen and paper. With this, she
took the sheet of paper with my writing on, scrunched it into
a ball, closed her eyes, inhaled deeply, clasped the crumpled

paper against her, then clearly and concisely projected the most awe-inspiring message I could ever have imagined

"You have the energy of a baby boy in your aura, and he is very close to you and has been for quite some time. He has been around many times before, and I am given the initial K with him."

As I struggled to comprehend the words I had just been given, I sat simply mesmerised and completely speechless! Thankfully the medium recognised my look of utter amazement and kindly took the time to explain herself. "Even if we don't know that we are pregnant or, if we realise but lose our child, whether it was at a week a month, two, five months or longer, the baby's spirit can often be seen in our aura."

I was completely and utterly gobsmacked. Wow! Just Wow! I would have been happy to finish the reading right there and then, as I had received more information than I could possibly have hoped for, but Kate wasn't ready to stop just yet. True to her word, the next round of information came forth like bullets from a gun, and I just about managed to keep up with her frantic pace.

There are far too many snippets to list, but she was spot on with almost everything. She also predicted that my eldest daughter would have a son and that my second daughter would have a girl first. Unfortunately neither are pregnant yet, so I shall have to wait patiently and see if these things transpire!

Once the seemingly endless stream of information had finally dried up, we turned to the photographs I had brought with me. Looking firstly at my Mum's picture, Kate announced that she also had the spirit of a baby boy around her. I was a little shocked at this suggestion as I was sure that I would have known if mum had lost a child. I wondered if she might be getting muddled up with my living brother, who Mum had been very close to, and gave the matter no further consideration.

While looking at my Nan's photograph, Kate stated that she had a George connected to her and an east London connection. I confirmed that George was indeed Nan's first husband, and the father of my dad and that yes, they also lived in the east end of London.

Finally, after studying my maternal grandparents' photograph for a few minutes, a flurry of information emerged, including a St James connection, a connection to Belfast, Ireland, a heart problem, and an underground tunnel where they pulled wood and coal in carts. I smiled and explained that my grandparents lived in James Street-James St, as it was mostly written on mail, and that there was also a St James' church very close to where they lived. My sister and I used to attend Girls Brigade (similar to Girl Guides) at the connecting St James Hall, and once a month we would go to the church. I think my mum may also have visited the church in her youth, as it was the closest one to her school. I later learned that my grandmother was buried in St James' churchyard. What a great piece of information to bring forward, I thought.

The Belfast connection was tied to my grandmother who was born and lived there before leaving Ireland to marry my granddad in the early 1930's. Sadly, my grandmother, Harriet, passed back in 1956 due to catching Rheumatic Fever and suffering Congestive Heart Failure, long before I was born.

I can only imagine that the mention of carts carrying coal was a reference to Harriet's father, my great-grandfather, Alex, who worked on the docks in Belfast, moving coal.

As the reading drew to a close, I once again, stopped to marvel at those first words. I was still in complete shock. What an amazing Easter gift I had been blessed with. Surely this was confirmation enough that the little boy I knew I was supposed to have, had in fact been with me for more than two decades! This absolutely fantastic revelation was going to take some time to process fully, but I walked out of that hall knowing that, (and not for the first time in recent years) my life would never be the same again!

I spent the following week in somewhat of a daze. The situation I found myself in was just so surreal. I wasn't quite sure how to proceed from here. On the one hand I was desperate to tell my husband, to tell somebody about my way out there experiences of late, but on the other hand, I could hardly believe it all myself. How on earth could I expect a sceptical husband-or anybody else for that matter, to make sense of it?

I needed to know more, I had to gather further

information before speaking out. I needed more validation and told myself that I would book just one more reading, this would be the last, then I would give the spirit world a rest. I did wonder if they might be despairing of me and my frequent disturbances!

PART FIVE

LIFTING THE VEIL

Chapter Eleven

THE BITTERSWEET TRUTH

Tears are the silent language of grief

– Voltaire

Brigid invited me into her home office and lit a candle, chatting as she did so, then explained that she used numerology as well as mediumship during her readings. After studying my husband and I's birth dates, Brigid proceeded to discuss vital areas such as health and business. She began with my husband and described his current work situation accurately and told me that his Scottish grandfather had stepped in with some advice for him.

At the time, this meant nothing to me, but I have since learned that my husband did indeed have a Scottish (great) grandfather, who passed when he was a baby. Brigid described some minor health issues that my husband had been experiencing and then moved on to me.

My Irish grandmother had joined us, and Brigid correctly

acknowledged that I look very much like her. She told me that I would go to Ireland in the next few years, that I would take an interest in my ancestors and that I would write a book. At that time, I had no plans to travel anywhere, let alone to Ireland which seemed at that point a million miles away. I had occasionally looked back over a few close generations of my family but had not gone into the matter in any depth and the idea of writing a book, while interesting, seemed completely unrealistic.

Yet, just three years on I have been tirelessly researching my family roots, thanks to being given a subscription to a genealogy site, for a birthday present, and have managed to uncover many generations of family members. To date, I have around two and a half thousand people in my family tree. I am heading off to Ireland for a holiday in five months' time and as for writing that book...

Heading back to the numerology once again, Brigid asked if I had any children so that we could check their birth dates and life path numbers. She must have thought me rather odd at this point, because I hesitated, laughed a little nervously, while all the time, unbeknownst to her I was cautioning myself to remain as secretive as possible so that I didn't lead her in any way...

"I do," I began, "but I'm not sure exactly how many I have" I hoped she didn't think that I was testing her unfairly!

"Alright," Brigid replied, "Let's ask them."

With this, she turned her head to the side as if having a silent conversation with somebody sitting next to her, then turned back to face me directly and with confidence and clarity stated:

"Five, you have five-boy, girl, girl, girl, girl, but the first one, the boy, you lost."

Five independent individuals had now spoken of a son. If they had mentioned a grandmother or grandfather figure with little else to back up their claims, that would have been pretty predictable, especially for a person of my age. It would have been a very safe relative to pick. A baby was not safe-and to name the specific gender of a baby at that, well that would have to be an incredibly risky guess. Yet five people had assuredly and without hesitation, confirmed the existence of a little boy, a son. Could this really be my Kieran, the little boy I knew I was going to become a mother to all of those years ago?

My head was thoroughly spinning, but my heart was brimming over with love for this little one who time and time again had taken the trouble to affirm his existence to me. Thank goodness he hadn't been deterred by my constant rejection at each mention of his presence. How frustrating each reading must have been as time and time again I denied him.

I felt terribly guilty and so very grateful that he had persevered and persisted until the penny had finally dropped for his non-believing mother. The power of unconditional love and devotion at its greatest!

As I continued to absorb everything that had been said to me, carrying on with my daily life while hiding such a huge secret inside, became unbearable. My initial feelings of joy, wonder and sheer amazement, were soon joined by those of realisation and pain, the deepest pain. I was of course so exceptionally grateful that my son and the spirit world had conspired to deliver me such a beautiful blessing of a gift.

To discover that I was a mother to yet another gorgeous child filled my heart with so much love. I felt truly blessed to have been given this opportunity and still do. I am incredibly thankful, but of course, in recognising that I had now found a son, I was faced with the knowledge that I had also lost a child. It was an awfully confusing situation that I found myself in and so very bittersweet.

It felt so wonderful to know that the little boy who had played such a silent but significant part in my life, was thriving, happy and very much around me, but I craved for the physical life that I had missed out on. I so desperately wanted to hold him and to kiss his little face, to witness his first smile, to hear his first words. I wanted to cheer and clap my hands with delight as he took his first wobbly steps towards me, then scoop him up in my arms and tell him what a clever boy he was. I had missed out on sharing the wonders of the world with him, missed out on observing the look in his eyes as he encountered his first animal or tasted his first ice cream.

I had missed out on every milestone and all of the magical moments in between, and it felt as if my heart had been smashed with a sledgehammer. At times the pain was so sharp that I could hardly catch my breath. I had lost many loved ones before but nothing compared to the torturous agony that I was now enduring, this was a loss like no other.

Despite physically losing my son all those years before, the pain felt so inconceivably raw and so immensely present! This was precisely the way I would have suffered at the time of his loss, had I known!

I felt overwhelmingly guilty that it had taken me quite so long to arrive at this point when surely I should have realised much earlier. Perhaps if I had been more open to believing in the afterlife, maybe he would have been able to reach through to me sooner. Had he been trying to attract my attention for more than twenty years? My head was still spinning and churning over, and over, a thousand Why's and What If's. I could no longer keep this incredibly irrepressible information to myself, I had to tell somebody.

My husband, like a lot of men, is a very logical and analytical kind of guy and I knew that he might struggle a little with the complete randomness of my news. It came as a momentous relief, when, after delivering the bombshell, he didn't raise his eyebrows or accuse me of being a crazy woman. While he probably didn't fully embrace the notion at that point, he nevertheless allowed me to speak without interruption, which was exactly what I needed.

Feeling uplifted by his calm semi-acceptance of the facts, I felt brave enough to broach the subject with two friends. The first, Margie, was completely supportive and shared my feeling of exhilaration at receiving such a precious revelation, she one hundred percent, completely and utterly got it, she empathised with my pain also and was wonderfully sensitive to all aspects of the news.

The second friend had unyielding views on the subject and wasn't afraid to voice them, and boy, did she voice them with a passion. Her response knocked me for six and silenced me in one fell swoop!

"Well it is quite sad, but it all happened so very long ago now, and if you didn't know anyway, why would you get so upset? I mean, it's not like you've got no other children is it? I suppose it's just a case of putting it behind you, moving on and not thinking about it too much, it's not like he was even born is it?"

To any parent who has ever been the victim of this type of blatant obliviousness and appalling disregard for your feelings, I am so sorry that you have had to be subjected to such a lack of compassion and basic human understanding. I really hope that, like me, this type of person can be the catalyst that drives you to speak your truth, however difficult, however controversial and unpopular it might be. Just as much as any other person's, your truth deserves to be heard. You deserve to be heard!

I procrastinated for far longer than was necessary before

deciding to share my story, and putting pen to paper. I did so because I was afraid of being judged, was worried about embarrassing my family, was scared of being misunderstood. Then it occurred to me that there might be other women, other men out there who felt the same way, and if I could help just one person to see that they were not alone, then, as terrifying as it was, I had to speak up.

Each and every life, no matter how brief, matters. Nobody has the right to devalue your feelings, your child existed- your child still exists. You are a mother, father, an aunt, or a grandparent and you always will be. Remembering and honouring your heavenly child is as natural as speaking of your earthly child, niece, nephew or grandchild. Please don't let those with absolutely zero experience or comprehension of your personal journey, make you feel that you ever have to suppress emotions or words.

Can You Feel Me, Mum?

> *The best and most beautiful things in the*
> *world cannot be seen or even touched, they*
> *must be felt with the heart*
>
> – Helen Keller

Since hearing from my son, I had developed an unquenchable thirst for all things spiritual and had acquired a very impressive stack of books on the topic, courtesy of my local library. I had selected a book from each of the most well-known and well-regarded authors of the genre, including Louise Hay, Doreen Virtue, and Dr Wayne Dyer to name just a few. I felt compelled to discover as much as I could about spirit communication and how I might be able to help my son to share further messages in the future.

I thought it best to take a break from booking any more readings for now, as I had come to understand that it requires a vast amount of energy for those in the spirit realm to connect with us. I didn't want my son to feel that he had to show up in order to keep Mum happy, especially if I was keeping him from some important heavenly work. Fortunately for me, my very determined boy had very different ideas.

"Do you fancy coming with us to a Psychic Fair?" asked my number three darling daughter one Friday evening.

"When you say, go with you, are you asking me to take you?" I teased, "I didn't think you believed in all of this airy fairy stuff?" Secretly I was rather amused and pleased that they may both have been becoming open minded to the possibility of there being more to this world than meets the eye.

"Well, it might be a laugh", my darling daughter number two responded, "But I might not be able to make it anyway as I've been invited out with friends" she warned. I doubted very much that she'd pick an afternoon with her 'way out there' mother over a fun time with her pals. I had completely dismissed the notion of going until the following morning when the girls asked what time we'd be leaving! Apparently, the outing with friends had been put on hold, and a couple of hours later, we were heading off to the nearby Hibiscus Coast.

I gave the girls some money and had a browse around the many stalls set up in the small church hall, by myself. There were some very fascinating books and a variety of Angel and Tarot cards in beautifully designed boxes, alongside stunning crystals, candles and jewellery. Stall holders were offering everything from Aura readings to Kinesiology healing.

By now, the girls had taken themselves off to have a clairvoyant reading each and were fully ensconced, so I headed over to the refreshment area and grabbed the last available seat. I hadn't been there for more than five minutes when a lady sat down in the newly vacant seat beside me and asked: "Are you waiting for me?" I looked at her and then glanced quickly down at the table only to see a box of Tarot cards and a pen and paper positioned directly in front of her. The penny dropped, she was a reader! I could have refused, I had decided to delay further readings for the foreseeable future after all, hadn't I? All resolve and will power quickly deserted me at that very moment I'm afraid, as I found myself uttering the words "Yes I am."

We introduced ourselves, and Tracey handed me the deck of cards to shuffle. As I began handling the cards, Tracey tuned into my energy and the following, most incredible reading took place:

Tracey "I am picking up on the energy of a teenage boy, I

would say around 18 or 19, he is very strong and won't let anybody else in! He is so very energetically strong and feels like he is, yes, he is your son."

Me "Wow, I have such intense goosebumps running up and down my spine. Oh wow! Am I feeling him too?"

Tracey "Absolutely! He is very close to you, and is determined to say what he needs to say"

Me "Good for him, that's fantastic!"

Tracey "He is telling me that you have been through some tough times, in the past five years specifically, he says it's been an uphill struggle for you at times. He's showing me a rose bud that is slowly opening up and is asking you to *Stop to smell the fragrance Mum*. He says this is a time of healing for you, everything is playing out as it should be, the time is right. It's time to look at the situation in its fullness and to heal from it, so a kind of closure... *Keep going Mum, keep persevering.*"

Me "Thank you, that's lovely."

Tracey "He wants to be acknowledged, he says you will understand what this means."

Me "Yes I do."

Tracey "He says that you have felt that he is around you, you think you may be getting signs from him, but you tell yourself that it's just your imagination."

Me (laughing) "Yes, that's right. I was sitting at the computer last night, and the light above me flickered a few times, then stopped and I did wonder if it might be him. I have been getting powerful goosebumps up and down my spine and even into my legs, at times when I am thinking about him a lot."

Tracey "It was definitely your son, he's laughing and asking, *Can you feel me, Mum?"*

Me (wiping away a tear) "That's so amazing! Thank you, that is just incredible."

Tracey "Do you have a brother in spirit?"

Me "No."

Tracey "He's just told me that his Uncle is here."

Me "I do have Uncles myself in spirit, my mum's two brothers Dave and Jim and my Godfather-Uncle Bill, could he be referring to one of those?"

Tracey "It feels more like his Uncle than yours. Not to worry if it doesn't fit we won't force things. He is telling me that you've felt a bit lost at times, and is asking you to take time for yourself, he says you are always helping others, but you need to take some time for yourself. He and the others in the spirit world will carry you. He sends you so much love. He's just so pleased to be here with you."

Me "That's a relief as I was worried I might be asking too much of him."

Tracey (laughing) "No way! He was determined to come through for you, he pushed through the crowd of your spirit family, and you have a lot of family here! and asked them all to step aside because he needed to speak to Mum."

Me "Bless him, I'm so pleased that he did! Thank you so much."

Once the reading had concluded, I thanked Tracey again for helping me to be part of such a fabulous and enlightening exchange. I was thoroughly blown away by my son's participation throughout the reading, and I found the whole experience incredibly moving. One thing puzzled me, however, the fact that my son had presented as a teenager, especially as I had lost him pre-birth. I could only have been between six and eight weeks pregnant at the time. Tracey explained...

"Once in spirit, a soul can choose to present at any age, up to their natural earth age, for example, a grandmother who passed at eighty years could present as an 80-year-old or might like to come through as she was in her thirties or even her twenties! Often a spirit presents themselves at an age that held fond memories for them - or for us. So how did you feel at eighteen or nineteen?"

Me "I was very free, had no responsibilities, no worries, yes it was a good time in my life."

Tracey "Although he passed before birth in this lifetime, he is an evolved soul, which means that he would have been here many times before. He has come through to you before right?"

Me "Yes, four times but I never actually allowed him to speak."

Tracey "I guess that he came through as a baby first?"

Me "Yes he did."

Tracey "He did that so that you would recognise him. I mean to say, if he came through as a teenager or twenty-something in his first ever reading, you would be wondering what on earth the reader was talking about. You would no doubt be telling him or her that you hadn't lost a teenage or adult child. This way, you had time to work it out, and I believe that your son wanted to give you a chance to catch up, to accept him as a baby and then a small child and so on, that way you could experience the different stages. Do you have other children?"

Me "Yes, I have four daughters."

Tracey "How lovely, I'm seeing a picture of 'Little Women', you have four beautiful and talented girls there, how old are they?"

Me "Twenty, eighteen, fifteen and eleven."

Tracey "I also think that your son wants you to know that he has grown, just as his sisters have, he has been with you all the time."

Me "That's so lovely, thank you. I have read a few books about reincarnation, and understand that many lost babies reincarnate as a subsequent child in the same family. I also read a book about parent's recollections of children's conversations, in which they casually mentioned how pleased they were to have stayed in their mother's tummies second time around because the first time wasn't right. Some decided to come back at a different time instead. I wonder why my son chose to remain in spirit rather than to come back as one of his sisters? (a slight pause) Oh Wow! I think I know why... if he'd come straight around again, I'd never have known it was him. I wouldn't have known he'd returned because I hadn't realised he'd left in the first place!"

Tracey "That's right, your son is going to stay with you, he chose to stay with you. He also wants you to know that you did nothing wrong, nothing at all and he loves you so much."

Me "Thank you, what a bright, gorgeous boy I have. I love him too, with all my heart."

Tracey "He is, and he has had many incarnations. He has so much love and admiration for you. He is insisting that you have nothing to feel guilty for, does this make sense to you? It is very important that I convey this"

Me "It makes perfect sense, thank you."

PART SIX

DELIVERED WITH LOVE FROM ABOVE

Chapter Twelve

MORE CELESTIAL SURPRISES

*He who looks outside dreams, He who looks
inside awakes*

- C Jung

One lazy Sunday afternoon, as I stood washing the dishes
and gazing out of the kitchen window at the beautiful
countryside view before me, it suddenly hit me. The
something missing feeling I had failed to escape from for
so long, had disappeared, it had completely vanished! I no
longer felt the presence of the dark cloud hovering above me,
it was quite extraordinary, without even noticing, something
quite profound had happened.

I felt a gigantic shift and a lightness where once the
opposite had been. I had no idea how or why, but for the first
time in seven long years, I finally felt settled. I no longer felt
homesick and the desperate urge to get back to England that
had crippled me for so long had totally dissolved. I searched

in vain for answers. I just could not explain it. And then, it occurred to me that, perhaps in finding my son, I had also found 'home'. It certainly felt as if my soul was rejoicing!

Life had not been dull, and the year 2013 was certainly going to go down in my personal history, as a year jam packed full of surprises.

As Christmas neared, I found myself thinking about my son and all of my wonderful family members in spirit. Every year, since Mum had passed, I had performed a series of rituals in her honour and in remembrance of her. This Christmas, I wanted to do the same for my son. I hadn't forgotten Tracey's message that my son wanted to be acknowledged. I took this to mean that he wanted others to know of his existence and that he probably wanted to be referred to by his name rather than just 'my son'!

A few days before Christmas, I bought a blue helium balloon with a butterfly design on it, and attached a handwritten note which began 'Darling Kieran'. Once the message was complete, I sent it up to heaven with a kiss and all of my love. On Christmas Eve, accompanied by two of my daughters, I visited the stunning Holy Trinity Cathedral here in Auckland. While the girls lit candles for their Nanny, Grandma and Aunty, I lit an extremely overdue one for my son and thanked him with all my heart, for giving me the best Christmas present imaginable.

Moving into 2014, it had been several months since I'd had a reading and I was itching to have contact with my son once more. I asked my friend Ellen if she would recommend somebody, which she kindly did, and the following week, Jill, a medium, arrived at my home. It was the first reading I'd had in the house, so I prepared a quiet place, lit a candle and invited anybody and everybody from my spirit family to come through. The doorbell rang, and I quickly removed all photographs from the room so as not to give any visual clues.

Jill "I've had a young man with me throughout the car journey here, he's been very excited and told me that *we're going to see Mum*. I know this must be a silly question now that I have said this, but have you lost a son?"

Me "Yes, I have."

Jill "It all makes perfect sense then, he seemed very pleased that I drove here in my husband's truck. He's very keen on it! He has a bunch of yellow roses for you, oh and I have to explain that they are in a box (laughing) it's crucial that I mention the box!"

Me (also laughing now) "Thank you, they sound beautiful, and the box sounds lovely too."

Jill "He's gorgeous, so excited to be with you, he is telling me how proud he is of you and how much he loves you. He's telling me *This is my mum, isn't she great?!"*

Me "That's so lovely, thank you, he is wonderful too!"

Jill "He is also telling me that he sleeps on the end of your bed and that you have felt him there..."

Me "Really? I don't think, oh actually, hang on a minute, I do remember something that happened a few months back. My husband and I were in bed, and the duvet at the end of the bed moved a few times, it was as if somebody was lifting it. I told my husband off for fidgeting, and he replied that it wasn't him and that he thought it was me! The movement continued for a few seconds, it frightened the life out of us. It was very odd."

Jill "He's laughing, *It was me, Mum*, he's saying."

Me "I'm so pleased to hear that! We were so freaked out by it. You are very welcome to sleep there anytime, though."

Jill "He is blowing you kisses, he's going to be with you until the end, he's with you twenty-four seven. He's telling me he's your number One and seems very pleased about this, and he keeps saying-*Number One.*"

Me "He is my eldest, he has four younger sisters."

Jill "He's laughing and saying that he's glad you didn't have another boy-he wants to be your number one and only boy!"

Me (laughing) "Well he certainly is that! Thank you."

Jill "He is such a happy chappy, he adores his sisters and has been looking out for them. One of them senses him."

Me "My eldest daughter has experienced some odd sensations in her room as if somebody was with her, and quite often the dog barks, and just stares as if she is seeing something/somebody, but there's nothing there. It's very spooky."

Jill "It's your son, oh and he loves the dog, he says she's crazy, though."

Me "Yes, she is. Very crazy indeed!"

Jill "I also have an older gentleman stepping in, he is giving me the name George, and he has a problem with his back."

Me "My granddad's name was George, and he was in the army and had to leave because he was wounded, I'm not sure how, though"

Jill "He is asking me to thank you."

Me "I don't know why, sadly I never got to meet him, he was my Nan's first husband, and after the war, they separated and later divorced. My dad didn't get to see him again, it was a very upsetting situation."

Jill "He said you have been helping people to remember him, have you been talking about him recently?"

Me "I have been researching my family tree and have just found a second cousin of my father, who has been filling in some blanks for me regarding that side of the clan, Oh and I've also sent off for granddad George's war records."

Jill "He's really pleased and grateful, he says 'it's lovely to be remembered and nice that somebody is thinking of me."

Me "He's very welcome, I feel very close to Granddad, even though we didn't get to meet"

Jill "I also have a quiet lady with sunglasses. '*Nana,*' is this your mum? I feel as if she is your son's Nana."

Me "Yes, my mum is in spirit."

Jill "She says that you are a good daughter, that you've had a bit of a rough ride at times but that you are doing well. Like a gentle warrior, you keep focused and keep going, you have been carrying a lot but have great inner strength, don't let the girls take advantage of you, she is saying that you do a lot for them. Make some time for yourself too! Don't forget to make time for date nights with hubby as well. She wants you to go out for dinner, just the two of you. She's showing me her legs, did she like them?"

Me "Ha-ha, yes she did have great legs, she loved dancing too"

Jill "Did one of your girls have a big, really tall, giraffe toy? I think it's the youngest daughter."

Me "Yes, yes she did, and Mum brought it for her. It was made of wood and stood by her bed. I'd completely forgotten about it."

Jill "I think you might have had a very romantic past life in France. A photo of Marie Antoinette has popped up, it looks like you were in the aristocracy."

Me (laughing) "That sounds very grand. Are you sure I wasn't a servant?! I have recently uncovered some French ancestor's actually. I had no idea that there were any French people in the family, so it came as a big surprise to discover that some of my great-grandparents hail from there. Sadly, they were refugees-Huguenots, who had to flee France for religious reasons or face persecution.

The funny thing is that I have always had a real fascination for France. I studied French at school and was never very skilled at writing, but seemed to pick up the accent and reading of the language quickly. I remember my French teacher asking me if I had any French relations, which really surprised and delighted me and I, of course, said no because I didn't think I had then. I have been to France a few times. Ireland and France are the two countries that have a real pull for me. It's very odd."

Jill "That's awesome! Past life connections with ancestors proven to be from these places. That is so great! And to have picked up the accent and pronunciation so easily and convincingly too, really makes me certain that you have had at least one past life there."

Me 'Thank You, it would explain a lot."

Jill "It would indeed. Lorraine, do you have a brother in spirit?"

Me "No."

Jill (pausing) "He's telling me his Uncle is there, but he's all grown up now. Are you thinking of writing a book about your Genealogy research? I believe that it would be a great idea."

Me "I have been meaning to put some printed records into files or books but haven't got around to it yet, I will do that then."

Jill "There is talk of a big secret, but we aren't allowed to say what it is. I think it's connected to your eldest daughter."

Me "She has been with her boyfriend for six years now, and they have been talking about getting married."

Jill "It might be time to buy a big hat. There is also a baby boy around her-not yet, though, don't worry!"

Me "How funny, you're the second person to say that."

Jill continued to discuss my daughters, and various predictions arose which I am keenly keeping an eye out for!

A new year and a new sibling

> *Where there is love, there is life*
>
> – Mahatma Gandhi

My father, Brian, flew out to Auckland every other year and spent a month or so with us and 2014 was to be no exception. At seventy-seven years of age, he did well to endure the very long and arduous journey alone, and I looked forward to his visits for months in advance. I had decided to tell him about my son, and I must admit that I was a little nervous as to exactly how he might react.

Dad is very old school in many ways and tales of the unexpected don't always sit well with him. Ironically, he has revealed to me that some thirty years or so previously, he experienced a very strange happening himself. One night, while lying in bed, he heard the rattling of chains and then observed an army of Roman Centurions marching, two by two, and as he watched them moving forwards, he noticed that they were only visible from waist height upwards. He could see no legs, yet they were undeniably marching! This incident shook him up, but he discounted it very quickly as being nothing more than a dream.

Interestingly, sometime after the dream occurred, a Roman coffin was discovered at one end of my father's road, and other areas close by had been excavated with a massive treasure trove of Roman artefacts being unearthed.

In the recent past, Dad has admitted to having further unexplained occurrences and has also experienced the feeling of being watched and sometimes feeling as if he is being touched on the arm or forehead. Whenever I probe further, Dad immediately dismisses the news as "Probably just my imagination," which of course it may well be, but it amuses me how he so obviously feels the need to bring everything back to a logical explanation, despite undeniably sensing these things.

My father had been staying with us for just over a week and appeared to have fully recovered from all of the associated symptoms of jet lag. We arranged to visit his favourite Auckland landmark, the imposing Sky Tower, a sixty storey, 328-metre high construction in the centre of the city. I had booked a table for us at the revolving restaurant there, which affords a magnificent 360-degree view over the city and far beyond as it slowly rotates. I thought that I would share my recent discoveries with Dad in a relaxed setting.

Apprehension had started to take hold of me, but I wanted my son to be acknowledged by more family members, having since told my sister and a couple of other close relations, who met the news with varying degrees of acceptance. Some were open and, while surprised, were willing to accept the situation, while others were, somewhat concerned with my mental state and wellbeing! I tried not to take things personally, but it did upset me when they struggled to see why I would be quite so affected after "all this time."

We ordered lunch and Dad took several photos, through the unrestricted glass windows. A bungee jumper hanging outside, paused for a few seconds, quite close to our table, before plunging to the ground below. My stomach turned a somersault, and the experience did nothing to calm my already somewhat inflamed nerves! I pondered silently, how would I begin? Which words would best convey my incredible news? My thoughts were interrupted by the arrival of our food, and then, after taking a very long, extremely deep breath, I decided that it was now or never!

The conversation went much better than anticipated, and I felt hugely relieved that Dad had allowed me to explain and to fully complete the long list of incidences without stopping me in mid flow. I sensed that he might have struggled a little with the details, but he was very sympathetic to the facts, which was exactly what I had hoped for from him. Once I had finished speaking, I noticed that Dad was looking very pensive. I attributed this to my inordinate news, but little did I know that he had a bombshell to deliver, all of his own!

Dad "Mum had a miscarriage before Sue was born."

Me "Really? She never mentioned it to me?"

Dad "I suppose there was no reason to do so."

Me "Was she very far gone, I mean, was it a late miscarriage?"

Dad "No, I don't think so, though I can't really remember. I believe that it was an early one, but she was staying with her sister at the time that she lost the baby. Do you know I can't remember!"

Me "So I don't suppose the gender was known?"

Dad "No, I don't think so."

I was completely dumbfounded, I had always been very close to my mother but knew nothing about this. I was utterly shocked that she had never shared this news with me. But on reflection, I guess that the only time Mum and I would ever have discussed pregnancy would have been when I was expecting each of my daughters and bringing up such a devastating fact at those times would have been incredibly anxiety provoking and insensitive of course.

Struggling to piece everything together, I wondered how such a major part of our family history could have been kept hidden for almost fifty years.

Suddenly, I recalled the occasions in which two different mediums had questioned me regarding the existence of an uncle to my son, or a brother to me, in spirit. Hadn't Kate, in my very first reading, also seen that Mum had the spirit of a baby boy around her? My sister and I, as children, had always discussed how great it would have been to have had a big brother, and I'm pretty sure that, at times, we included a fictitious one in many of our games.

Could my older sibling in spirit, also have been the invisible playmate I had spent so much time with in my formative years?

Me "I think I know the gender. The baby was a boy, and the boy is now a grown man!"

I had now been hit with a second revelation of almost equal breathtaking proportion as the first. Not only had I learned of the existence of a son, but I had also acquired a new sibling in spirit!

What an unquestionable phenomenal confirmation that our loved ones continue to live on in the afterlife, and how amazing it is to learn that, even those who were not able to be with us in this physical life, remain with us in the spiritual-even those we knew absolutely nothing about!

My mum was extremely close to her elder sister, Ivy, and two years after the conversation with my father had taken place, my sister paid a visit to our aunt. Another revelation was uncovered that day, and we were stunned to learn that Mum's miscarriage hadn't occurred quite as early as we had believed. She had in fact known that her lost child was a boy. Further confirmation indeed!

Chapter Thirteen

MAD DOGS AND DANCING SHOES

*Death has nothing to do with going away. The
sun sets, the moon sets, but they are not gone*

– Rumi

One summer morning, while driving my two youngest daughters to school, old and new hits, courtesy of the car radio, accompanied us as we drove along the country roads. Veering widely in order to overtake a labouring tractor which was chugging painfully slowly uphill, my concentration was instantly alerted to a segment being broadcast from the local radio station. Reaching for the volume button, and increasing the sound rapidly, I listened intently as the radio host interviewing a guest medium, invited listeners to call in for a free mini reading.

We had just reached school by the time that the participant's questions were being aired, so I pulled over and waved my daughters off, watching as they made their way inside the school building. Reaching for the volume button once again, I sat for a few minutes, listening to one caller after another receiving advice and insight into a wide variety of issues including romance, business and health. The first volunteer seemed particularly pleased to hear that the man she had been nothing more than 'just good friends' with for almost three years, was in fact interested in her romantically, just as she was in him. I really hoped the medium had got that right!

I settled into my seat and became fully immersed in each interaction. As the segment drew to a close, the radio host turned his attention to the medium herself and requested that she share her history with the masses. Mary explained that she had been aware of her gift from a young age, and later went on to study at the prestigious Arthur Findlay College of Spirituality and Psychic Sciences, in England.

This snippet of information impressed me tremendously because I had heard great things about the place, which has been likened to 'Hogwarts'- a reference to the fictitious school of wizardry from the Harry Potter series of books and films. I also knew that famous British mediums such as the late Colin Fry and Lisa Williams had studied at the college. It has a fantastic reputation amongst those in the spiritual arena.

I wondered how expensive this lady's readings might be, I guessed that she would be completely out of my price range, but thought I'd check online once home, after all, it had been a while since my last reading, and let's face it, I don't need much encouragement to check in with that gorgeous son of mine!

Perhaps Kieran himself had led me to select this particular radio station today. I frequently flick from station to station to avoid the morning chat and news shows, in search of a good song or two, yet, breaking the habit of a lifetime, I had ended my search this morning at just one of those easily avoidable and usually dull talk shows. As I pondered further, the sight of a passing car gave further credence to my son's possible involvement as the number plate ISONI brought a smile to my face.

Three weeks later, Mary shook my hand and welcomed me into her beautiful home by the sea. The view from her home office/healing room was breathtaking, and I imagined that laying on her healing table, watching the waves lap gently just outside of the window, must offer a beautifully tranquil and therapeutic experience for her clients. I took a seat, and as Mary prepared the sound equipment, in readiness for recording the session, I admired her stunning collection of crystals and made myself comfortable.

Mary "I have a lady here who is very insistent on coming through, she feels like a mother, yes she tells me she is your mother and wants you to know that she is still very much here. She is a bit agitated, she feels like she went before her time and wasn't completely ready to go and is saying *I'm still here you know*!"

Me "That is so spot on. Mum had only celebrated her 68th birthday a month before she passed and she was making plans the week before her passing, despite being in a hospice. She genuinely thought she had more time."

Mary "She is telling me about your dad. I take it they went through some bad times as she's telling me some home truths about him, did they separate a long time ago?"

Me (laughing) "Oh dear, yes there were certainly some fireworks between them! They divorced many years ago."

Mary "She is also telling me that your sister has been and is going back to France soon, and with a boyfriend, is that right?"

Me "Wow! Yes, my sister's boyfriend has a house in France, and they have recently been staying there and are planning to return in a couple of months' time."

Mary "She is giving me some names of people you will know, Ivy, Lily, Teresa, Kathy, Sherryl-Lee."

Me "Ivy is my mum's eldest sister, Lily is an old friend of hers, Teresa is my mother in law, Kathy was a neighbour, I'm not sure why she'd mention her, Oh yes, I do know a much more significant and lovely lady called Kathy! Sherryl-Lee is my daughter's piano teacher. Mum loved the piano, but her parents could never afford to pay for lessons, so she was very pleased when two of my daughters showed an interest. Thank you, those names are fantastic!"

Mary "She is very pleased and tells me that you have a walnut coloured piano at home, is that right?"

Me "Yes, yes we do. I expect she will be telling me off now because it needs tuning!"

Mary "No, you're ok, who is the teacher in the family? Mum says they will be doing some great teaching."

Me "I don't, oh wait, my eldest daughter is training to be a teacher!"

Mary "The little one likes basketball."

Me "I'm not sure what this means, I know mum used to like playing netball."

Side note: A few weeks after my appointment with Mary, my youngest daughter came home from school with a form that I needed to sign, giving permission for her to join the girls' basketball team.

This came completely out of the blue as she had never mentioned anything about liking the sport before. Sure enough, she went on to join the team and even made it to the 7.15 a.m. weekly practice sessions without complaint, and I like to think that her Nanny was watching over her at each of her games.

Mary "She has a son too, did they have a falling out towards the end? She wants to say she is sorry and wants to make up."

Me "Yes, she was very close to my brother, but, sadly, they fell out just a week or two before she went into the hospice and the two didn't speak again before she passed."

Mary "Was she a smoker? She is saying that smoking didn't help her health. She is also telling me that she came to see you and had stripes in her hair, what does that mean?"

Me "Yes, she was a smoker, she did give up some years before she passed but I think the damage had already been done. As for the stripes, I'm not sure, oh hang on, when she came over to visit me, her one and only trip to New Zealand, she had some highlights in her hair which I hadn't seen. This was the first time she'd ever had her hair highlighted."

Mary "Sorry, I should have realised that she meant highlights. She is showing me something else now, and this might seem a bit odd, but she liked her shoes didn't she?"

Me "Yes she did, she was always very glamorous and loved her shoes to match her outfit."

Side note: As Mary mentioned Mum's shoes, I could clearly picture her, sitting in a chair, dressed to the nines, reaching down to secure the buckle on her favourite pair of black, leather, Mary-Jane shoes. I recalled the exact ones because I longed to have a similar pair, but standing at just under six feet tall in bare feet, I could only dream of wearing such a pair of heels! As I held the image in my mind, Mary astounded me by reaching down to secure the buckle on a pair of imaginary shoes, in precisely the way that Mum did!

Mary "She is showing me a pair of shoes and is reaching down to fasten the buckle."

Me "Oh my, this is so crazy! As you mentioned shoes, I saw exactly what you just described, ooh I'm getting goose bumps!"

Mary (smiling) "The spirit's like to prove to us the existence of life after death, this was Mum's way of doing so. She gave you a pretty everyday scenario, but one that had great significance for you, one that would stir up a vivid memory in your mind."

Me "That's amazing! Thank you."

Mary "Who is the M connection, I feel a very strong M joined to you, not in spirit, though"

Me "Could it be my husband-Mark?"

Mary "Yes! You two are very connected."

Me "We've been together for 27 years."

Mary "Mum has softened a lot now, she is at peace. She will send you roses, red roses, as signs that she is around you."

Me "I have planted a red rose bush for her in the garden."

Mary "She sends lots of love to you and says you are her hero. I am picking up on another energy now, a young male, who is Keen Kier Kieran?"

Me "Oh my goodness! That's my son, Kieran."

Mary "He has been waiting so patiently for Mum to finish speaking, he's lovely and is telling me that you love purple, no, that you *really* love purple! You have lots of it around?"

Me (laughing) "Absolutely correct. I love everything purple and usually always have something purple on me and frequently wear purple-except for today though which is very unusual for me. That is just brilliant. Everybody that knows me well knows that I am a purple addict."

Mary "He says that you have a dog and that she's a little crazy."

Me "Yes, we do, and she is very boisterous and a jumpy kind of dog, unfortunately. We all love her, though."

Mary "He likes planes and looks almost angelic. Your son is ethereal looking and is completely content. He sends butterflies as signs for you and has lighter rather than darker hair and a mole on his cheek."

Me "That's so wonderful, I call him my butterfly and my angel and have a blue butterfly in my bedroom for him, and also a butterfly candle. My eldest daughter and my Mum both have moles on one cheek too."

Mary "Who is Lorri? He's giving me the name Lorri?"

Me "That's me, Lorri is my nickname-my dad always used to call me Lorri when I was young."

Mary "He tells me that you sometimes sense him and that you should know that he is one hundred percent here, it's not your imagination. He sends lots of love too and also tells me that you are his hero, so please don't worry, you did nothing wrong. Nothing at all. He is always close to you. They are saying it's very sad about your sister in law, it was such a terrible thing."

Me "Thank you, I love him too, and he is without a doubt, my hero. Mum too. We lost my sister in law at just 25, it was awful."

Mary "That is so tragic. I get the strong impression that, although you are a believer in the afterlife, you have many people around you who aren't, is that right?"

Me "Yes definitely! I have to be very careful, particularly around some members of my wider family who feel that I may have lost the plot at worst and that I'm obsessed with all things spiritual at best."

Mary "It isn't an easy position to be in, and I understand completely. All you can do is to hold on to your experiences, they are your proof. Some people are afraid of things that they don't understand or can't explain, but you have to follow your heart. One last thing, Mum, is telling you to buy some proper footwear, do you have a problem with your shoes?"

Me (laughing) "I always used to try to squeeze my feet into pointed shoes when I was a teenager but got so many blisters. Mum would always tell me that I should look after my feet. I recently bought a pair of shoes, and they have given me blisters. Ok, Mum, I will throw them away and will buy a more sensible pair!"

Mary "She's very pleased to hear this. I also have your grandfather here. He is showing me little Prince George, William and Kate's son."

Me 'My granddad's name is George. Sadly I never got to meet him."

Mary "He is very fond of you, he loves you and is grateful that you are keeping his memory alive. He has asked me to let you know that he is absolutely fine and that the past is all just a blur now, so please don't worry. He is very happy and is showing me something which is making him laugh, it is a cauldron. He said that you will see the funny side. He is acknowledging that you have the gift, he says you are a lovely witch!'"

Me (laughing) 'That's so funny. It has been suggested by a few mediums, that I was a 'see-er' in a past life. Not one of them has put it quite so bluntly though. It's alright Granddad, I often refer to myself as a witch too-a white witch, though."

As we completed the reading, I sat in total awe at the evidence presented to me and revelled for a few moments in the magnificent realisation that there is so very much more to this life than meets the eye. How thoroughly amazing it is to know that our loved ones are never more than a breath away from us. Mary provided some further information with me that is too personal to share here, but her words gave further credence to my mother, grandfather and son being very much present throughout the reading.

PART SEVEN

WORKING TOWARDS
HEALING OUR HEARTS

Chapter Fourteen

PSYCHIC CLAIRVOYANT OR MEDIUM, WHICH SHOULD I CHOOSE?

We are not human beings having a spiritual experience. We are spiritual beings having a human experience

– Pierre Teilhard de Chardin

While Dad was with me, we talked in-depth about the different types of reader and readings that exist. He offered me his take on things, suggesting that a huge number are charlatans, but conceded that there were probably some excellent ones out there also, none more so than the wonderful earth angels I'd been fortunate enough to encounter over the past year.

I welcomed his cynicism because I do think that it is important to receive detailed, accurate information and to feel genuinely satisfied with the facts being presented. This is what sets the naturally gifted mediums and clairvoyants apart from the rest. I do, however, believe that if a person arranges a reading and expects 100% accuracy or specifies that a particular loved one should appear, that they are setting themselves up for disappointment.

Of course, it is perfectly acceptable to ask for our loved ones to come through for us, but we mustn't be despondent if Great Granny Georgina doesn't make it to the reading. There may be a number of reasons why a certain loved one doesn't make contact in a reading, perhaps other loved ones have information that needs to be passed on more urgently, or possibly Granny's energy may be more challenging to decipher, at this moment in time. It doesn't mean that she won't come through for you in a subsequent reading.

Looking back, there were snippets of information that I couldn't place, in one of my readings, but the unarguably accurate information handed to me, more than made up for those. As I reflected on each of my readings, I began considering the best way to approach a potential reader and how I might be able to help the session to progress. I have listed some tips that may help a person seeking a spiritual reading to get the best out of the meeting.

Firstly, perhaps it might be helpful to explain the different types of readers available, as I know that I was very confused with the various options, and totally unsure whether or not to choose a psychic clairvoyant or a medium - aren't they both the same thing I questioned? Apparently not!

A *Clairvoyant,* (From the French words of Clair, meaning *clear* - and Voyant, *viewing,* or *seeing)* is the name given to a person with psychic powers, who can clearly see things that most of us can't. There are several types of Clair or clear, and these include:

Clairaudience, which is the ability to have clear hearing. So, the ability to receive words and sounds from Spirit into the inner ear or mind.

Clairsentience, the ability to clearly sense or to feel, and to gain information through a feeling that occurs within the whole body.

Clairtangency, this is better known as Psychometry and means the ability to sense information by touch. This is usually carried out by touching or holding an inanimate object, such as a piece of jewellery.

Clairgustance, which means clear taste, the ability to taste without having a physical substance in the mouth.

Clairscent, Some people are also able to smell a certain aroma, which is not present, for example, tobacco smoke, a fragrant flower or a particular perfume to name a few.

A Clairvoyant can connect to a person's soul by reading the energy field, or aura, surrounding them. A gifted clairvoyant is able to produce information from the client's past, present and often, their future.

A Medium is a person who can connect with loved ones who have passed on and then transmits information from spirit and relays it to somebody on the earthly plane, usually with the help of a spirit guide. Just as an old radio often requires fine-tuning to find the correct frequency and wavelength, a medium has the tricky job of raising her energetic vibration to match that of the spirit and then needs to decipher and to deliver facts in a way that can be understood by the person she/he is reading for. I would imagine it is a bit like Chinese whispers, with some information perhaps being understandably lost in translation!

All mediums possess psychic powers, while some clairvoyants also have the ability to connect with spirit, but usually they are stronger in one aspect than the other.

Both clairvoyants and mediums are often able to read Angel or Tarot cards, and some are trained to use Astrology, Psychometry or Numerology in their readings.

So who is best? Well, that really depends on your reason for booking a reading. If I wanted to gain some insight into my career path or needed help with deciding whether or not it was a favourable time to sell my house for example, then I think I'd choose the clairvoyant. If on the other hand, I was eager to hear from my loved ones in spirit, then I would book to see the medium.

If you are unsure which one to choose, ask a prospective reader what type of information is likely to be shared with you. Better still, and I would strongly advocate doing this whenever possible, ask friends, family or colleagues for recommendations. This way, you can learn in advance how things are likely to proceed and can gain valuable tips before the reading takes place.

Many mediums and clairvoyants also offer email, phone and Skype readings. It isn't necessary to meet in person, and readings can be undertaken no matter how great the distance between reader and client. I would strongly advise against using any '0800 Dial a Psychic' type of services that are advertised online as I suspect that these are a scam.

A personal recommendation should always be the first go to, and it is essential that a person's credentials are checked beforehand, for your own safety. I, personally, would be very wary of choosing somebody with very limited or no public information or testimonials freely available to view, unless he/she was personally recommended by a friend or relative known to me who I trusted implicitly.

Once you have selected the most suitable person and you are ready to book the appointment, there are a few things to consider asking, for example, is an audio recording of the session provided? If not, is it possible to take along a recording device yourself? Will you be able to take notes? (This is a must if you do not have the audio option, as information will hopefully come flying at you which you may not manage to retain all of in the excitement!) Also, it's good to play back your reading, or to revisit your notes, to see what was actually said versus what you think you remember being said.

When you are happy to go ahead, pick a day and time

in which you have sufficient free time so that you are not rushing to or from the reading, this way, you will arrive relaxed and calm. Also, it's a good idea to allow yourself some time to process everything afterwards, without interruption. If you suspect that you will be feeling nervous, ask the reader if it is acceptable to take a friend along with you.

Most mediums and clairvoyants should be happy to accommodate such a request and the great thing about having a second pair of ears in the room is that you are likely to gather more information between the two of you. A friend could also jot down notes while giving you the chance to listen without multi-tasking.

Before each of my readings, I asked my loved ones to come through for me-if they were able to, that way I'd set the intention but wasn't expecting them to show up. I found that this grounded me and it meant that I wouldn't be too disappointed if I didn't receive a message from a spirit that I desperately wanted to hear from.

Once with the reader, I was very aware of not giving anything away, I didn't want to provide any clues but merely responded with a Yes, if the information relayed was accurate, or a No if things didn't make sense. I would say that it is crucial not to try to make things fit, and a simple 'I can't place this' will not cause offence.

Please don't sit through a reading without speaking up if you feel that the facts are not gelling together. I have a friend who sat through an hour long reading only to have a couple of very minor things given that made any sense to her. I asked why she didn't say something and she replied that she didn't like to interrupt!

If you are feeling that the reading is going this way for you, please speak up. Ten minutes should be long enough to find some common ground. In the event that no information is forthcoming, you are perfectly entitled to ask for a second free reading or a full refund.

Often, information given from spirit can be hard to fathom at times, and it might take a bit of detective work to get to the main message. In one of my readings, for example, I was asked if pasta was my favourite food, and apparently, my cheeky son was laughing as he suggested to the medium that she ask me this question.I do like pasta, but I can't say that it's my number one favourite, so I was a little taken aback and had to say so.

The medium then asked my son for more information and went on to explain that she could see a large pasta dish sitting on a kitchen bench alongside pots and pans, lots of mess and for some reason, a clock. It took me a second then I too laughed, because she was describing the scene in my kitchen the previous night!

I am not the greatest cook, and it has become a standing joke with my family, but I had decided to try out a new pasta recipe, which took me far longer than it should have done and left me feeling rather flustered as I struggled to get it into the oven before dinner time arrived. At one point I thought we'd be eating it for breakfast! I was in quite a grumpy mood by the end of the saga and vowed that I would never bother cooking anything exciting with pasta again.

If I had not spoken up, I would have put this part of the reading down to the medium taking an unlucky guess and wouldn't have been too impressed. By letting Lynda know that the message didn't sit with me, it meant that she could ask Kieran further questions and was able to clarify the situation.

Some information given in a reading, may not make sense immediately, so I like to refer to my notes or to play my recordings a few days afterwards to see if anything that seemed to be a miss at the time may now have become a hit. It's good to revisit notes some months later also.

As the session comes to a close, most readers will ask if you have any questions that you would like answered, so it is a good idea to go prepared with a few in mind. I can recall being asked at my very first reading and feeling as if I had been completely put on the spot. I could think of absolutely nothing to say. Of course, once home, a hundred and one things sprang to mind, and I was kicking myself!

Finally, I like to give feedback, if the reader has provided some great evidence and left you feeling happy and upbeat, then I think it's good to let them know. Equally, if your experience was not what you'd hoped for, then it is even more essential that you tell them. Don't be put off by one bad reading. However. There are many gifted people out there.

Chapter Fifteen

THE BRAVEST OF WARRIORS

*It takes a strong woman to be a mother, but it
takes an even stronger woman to be a grieving
mother*

– B J Karrer

As I have mentioned briefly before, I am a keen researcher of
all things historical and have become completely addicted to
anything and everything related to Genealogy. My mother's
maternal side of the family has proved to be decidedly
vexing to trace in that it has taken me eight years to collate
information for just three descending generations of family
members!

However, I am pleased that I struggled on to uncover the
treasures that I have recently unearthed. Even the distressing
and at times downright heartbreaking accounts of everyday
life in centuries long past has done nothing to deter me from
digging and delving.

After spending countless painstakingly long hours and years getting nowhere, I eventually encountered the breathtaking feeling of enlightenment. Data, more precious than diamonds, materialised, seemingly out of nowhere, and was once again shown the light of day. All memories of burning the candle at both ends in the hope of breaking through a brick wall, dispersed in an instant.

The thing that thrills me most about verifying such golden nuggets is that by doing so, I am afforded at worst, a glimpse, and at best, a complete appreciation of the character and strengths of my forebears, and I find this incredibly exhilarating! I have also been hugely moved in recent months, having exposed the devastating news that baby and child loss is something sadly only too familiar in my family lineage.

In the 1940's my maternal grandmother, Harriet, lost her first child to meningitis when he was just four years old. Nan was just a month away from giving birth to her fourth child and was also caring for my mother and her elder sister. I cannot imagine how she found the strength to carry on.

Back in 1900, my great-grandmother, Mary, lost her first child to miscarriage and later, in the 1930's, an adult child of 23 passed due to the effects of Typhoid.

Stepping back a little further in time, and in 1870, while eight months pregnant with her fifth child, my great- great-grandmother, Hannah, suffered the unimaginable heart-wrenching loss of three children, aged just two, four and six to Diphtheria. The children all passed, one after the other, in the space of just four weeks. I struggle to contemplate the immense anguish and torment that she must have felt, watching each of her three children slipping away from her, feeling inescapably helpless and just praying and pleading for the life of her last living child (my great-grandfather) who, thankfully, survived.

I am extremely proud of my grandmothers and of their strength and resilience which was more than tested to the core. I would not have blamed any one of them for wanting to give up or for completely losing their mind, but thankfully, somehow, they found the fortitude and courage to keep going. I am so inspired by these three strong women and feel incredibly blessed to be a part of their clan.

We, women, have endured having our babies torn away from us since the beginning of time. How sad it is to think that, in so many areas mankind has made colossal strides forward, regarding science and medicine, yet here we are in the year 2017, and babies and children are still being taken far too soon. It is vital that we are able to express ourselves with like-minded women and men who have also experienced the unthinkable.

With this in mind, I would like to honour another type of baby loss that has not yet been addressed. Sudden Infant Death Syndrome (SIDS) which is also commonly known as cot death. I have heard some absolutely horrendous stories around this subject

This type of loss, which is obviously both shocking and devastating, comes with a huge amount of trauma. Firstly, a mother is forced to deal with the inexplicable circumstances surrounding the loss of her child. As if this isn't enough to cope with, she is then subjected to the most harrowing of interrogations. I cannot imagine the agony a woman must go through in having to prove her innocence.

Yes, it is, of course, a very sad, but real fact that many babies die at the hands of their abusive parents, and of course, all unexplained infant deaths must be investigated, but many completely innocent parents are being treated in a disgraceful manner. Sensitivity and compassion need to be much more readily exercised around investigating this type of loss. My heart goes out to every parent who has lost a child in this way.

Whether a mother has lost her child to miscarriage, stillbirth, SIDS, disease, an accident or any other condition, the overriding desire in all cases is that her child is never forgotten. Regrettably, I have spoken with so many women whose wish has not been granted, and it is incredibly distressing to hear their agonising stories.

Many women who have experienced a very early miscarriage speak of being denied the right to grieve properly. The common thread between such women is that family and friends were supportive immediately after the loss but then moved on, after a very short period of time. Worst still, they also expected the bereaved mother to do the same. Because a funeral service and burial were out of the question, it was quite generally expected that the mother should recover immediately and never need to speak of her baby again.

I cannot think of anything crueller than to dismiss a bereaved parent's grief in this manner. Those whose lives have not been touched by child loss will never understand the deep yearning every bereaved mother has to keep her child's memory alive.

I recently discovered some quotes and poems that reveal just how common it is for bereaved parents to be ignored or made to feel that the loss of their little miracle should not be discussed because it makes others feel uncomfortable. Every parent has the utmost right to grieve and to remember their precious angel for as long as they choose to do so. Forever seems like a perfectly acceptable and ideal time frame to me!

I have heard such excuses as "Well, perhaps a person was afraid of saying the wrong thing and didn't want to cause upset." I suspect that this is true in many cases, but how about offering the gift of presence, to aid a grieving parent and to reassure them that they are not alone. Just showing up, sitting quietly and being there can be as equally healing as speaking the right words. If a person has the courage to confide in you with this, the most traumatic and devastating experience, would you not feel extremely honoured and privileged to have been afforded this personal truth? Is it too much to offer a kind "I'm so sorry, thank you for sharing this with me?"

Sadly, as we all know only too well, there is still a marathon of a way to go in raising awareness and educating those with absolutely no idea whatsoever!

*I've lost a child, I hear myself say, and the person I'm talking
to just turns away.*

Now why did I tell them? I don't understand,

It wasn't for sympathy or to get a helping hand.

I just want them to know, I've lost something dear.

I want them to know that my child was here.

My child left something behind which no one can see,

So, if I've upset you, I'm sorry as can be.

You'll have to forgive me, I could not resist,

I just want you to know that my child did exist.

- Author Unknown

Healing Creations

Perhaps you might like to write a poem or a quote for
your baby. Maybe you would like to start a journal or to
write a letter to your beloved child. I, personally, feel that
there is something very cathartic about putting my thoughts
onto paper. It is a wonderful source of expression and allows
for a great release of emotions. If you feel more of a pull
towards other creative outlets, for example, painting, drawing

or perhaps making a memento for your angel, or creating a beautiful area of remembrance in the garden or cemetery, or maybe a colourful window box, these are all very healing activities also.

Whatever you choose to create, remember that you don't have to produce a masterpiece and of course you may keep your work private if you do not feel comfortable sharing it with others.

It was suggested to me, by an amazing lady, who I have mentioned briefly and who will feature again later in the book, that I treat myself to some paints, brushes and paper because my son wanted to help guide me to produce a piece of artwork that would relate to him. She also added that he'd asked her not to suggest that we sketch as I would be put off immediately and might freeze in fear at the suggestion. I had to laugh. My son was spot on. My artistic ability is no doubt on par with that of a five-year-old. My match stick depictions of people are rather primitive, to say the least! Being asked to paint was fear provoking enough, but as long as I could keep my work to myself, then sure, I'd give it a whirl.

One sunny and calm Sunday afternoon, I set the garden table up as a mini art station, complete with pads, coloured pencils, pens, paint and brushes. I then invited my daughters to join me at 'Mum's Art Circle'.

My girls peeked quizzically out through the lounge window as if to say "What's all this about then?" It was completely out of character for me to get artsy!. With my youngest daughter now aged 13, it had been a few years since we had created childish works of art together.

The girl's curiosity soon got the better of them, fortunately, and they eventually came out to join me. While my young artists began generating easily recognisable representations of birds, butterflies and flowers, I sat for a moment and pondered my first move. So how was this going to work I wondered? I asked my son for help, and while everybody was absorbed in their activity, I closed my eyes, lifted my paint coated brush to the paper and began randomly making brush strokes. Pausing briefly to coat the brush once more, I continued to 'paint' until I felt that it was time to stop.

On opening my eyes, I was met with a rather abstract image which portrayed, well nothing in particular. As I scanned the fruits of my labour, I felt rather disappointed. The picture before me conveyed nothing heavenly and didn't resonate with me at all.

As I sat scrutinising, I heard or thought? I am not sure exactly which, but it felt as if somebody was speaking and advising me...*Turn the paper around so that it's in portrait, not landscape.* I followed the instruction and did as requested and, Wow! What a difference. Some of the brush strokes had made letter K's along the edge of the page, and at the centre, it appeared that two statues or figures were kneeling down, sideways on, the larger, taller one behind the smaller shorter one and they were both facing in the same direction.

Was this Kieran and I? The painting now had an entirely different vibe to it and resonated incredibly powerfully with me. I asked one of my daughters if she could see what I could and she confirmed that yes, she too could see the letter K's, which slightly resembled Chinese characters used in writing, and the two beings in the centre of the painting. My youngest daughter offered a somewhat different viewpoint, by suggesting that the two figures, if looked at from a slightly different angle, also resembled a foetus. My daughter knew nothing about my miscarriage at this point, and I must admit that I was quite taken aback by her accidental yet astonishingly insightful words. I was reminded of a particular phrase once more 'Out of the mouths of babes!'

I framed the painting, and it now sits in my bedroom, alongside photographs of my four daughters. I'm not entirely sure that others would see what my girls and I do, but I very much believe that my son helped to orchestrate the family art session and was with his sisters and I as we sat together and calmly composed our mini art collection.

I wrote this poem for my son and thought I'd share it with you:

Precious Gift

My butterfly, my angel, my saving grace,
Too beautiful for time or place.
You guide me gently, you light my way,
I feel you beside me every day.
Giver of hope, of love and joy,

A precious gift, my darling boy.

Rosebud pure as crisp white snow,

On earth, you had no time to grow,

To bloom in Heaven was the plan,

Blissfully, freely, amazing young man.

One day we'll get to lift the veil,

That separates, however frail.

I'll hold you in my arms at last,

Dissolve the pain that cloaks the past.

For now, each rainbow, sunset, star,

Reminds me that you're never far.

Your angelic presence lives in my heart,

Forever and always, and never to part.

Thank you, Kieran, for choosing no other,

I feel so blessed to be called your mother.

Lorraine E Stone.

PART EIGHT

HEAVENLY HELLOS

Chapter Sixteen

A CHANCE DISCOVERY LEADS TO FURTHER REVELATIONS

For life and death are one, even as the river
and the sea are one

– Khalil Gibran

As I drove to my local Supermarket one miserable, rainy morning, my windscreen wipers going nineteen to the dozen, a red light, on the dashboard, indicated that I was in imminent danger of breaking down at any given moment due to a lack of fuel. It glared angrily at me as if to say 'Here we go again, you've left it to the very last minute, will you ever learn?!' How a vehicle made of metal can possess the power to make a person feel quite so ashamed I really don't know.

At that moment, I did exactly as I have done, time and time again when finding myself in this situation, I began pleading for mercy! "If you could just let me make it to the nearest service station, I promise that I will never let the

petrol get so low again-ever! Honestly, please, pretty please"
By now, the fuel level gauge was completely off the dial, and
I wasn't sure how long it had been at absolute rock bottom.

Thankfully somebody was listening to me that morning,
and five minutes later the car was still moving. I finally
pulled up beside the most magnificent sight, a beautiful life
saver of a petrol pump. Turning the ignition off, I let out a
huge sigh of relief, and an almighty thank you!

Rummaging through the depths of my disorderly
handbag, for a fuel voucher that would offer me a meagre
saving on my purchase, the feeling of shame experienced
earlier crept back once again. When had I last given my bag
a good clean out? Far too long ago judging by the ancient
shopping lists, outdated coupons, discarded chewing gum
wrappers, empty lip balm containers and general debris
lurking in the depths of the unknown.

My hopeless search continued on in vain, and after what
seemed like an eternity, I finally resigned myself to the fact
that I would never find the voucher by wading through the
vast pile of rubbish in this manner. With this realisation, I
lifted the container disguised as my handbag up high and
tipped it upside down before aggressively shaking the relics
out onto the passenger seat beside me.

Looking up for a moment, I noticed the pump attendant
smiling nervously through the front windscreen at me, this
hoarder of a customer with the entire contents of a good-
sized bin stacked up beside her! Smiling sweetly, I grabbed
my credit card and raced into the shop, avoiding eye contact,

stopping only to call out "Fill her up please!" as I went. Perhaps I'd use the voucher another time.

Once home, with my handbag feeling considerably lighter than it had at the start of the day, I decided that perhaps it might be a good idea to give my wallet a decent spring clean also. While this turned out to be a less substantial project than the handbag clearance, I had also accumulated a wide variety of useless business cards, old loyalty cards for shops that were no longer trading and a host of faded, entirely illegible receipts. Tossing everything worthless into the recycling bin, I retrieved the cards and papers from the final, as yet unchecked, section of the wallet.

Between two receipts, I discovered a business card that I was sure I had never seen before. Where on earth had it come from? After much thought and deliberation, I suddenly recalled my visit to the Spiritualist church, a few years earlier. At the entrance to the hall, a table with mediums, clairvoyants and healers business cards greeted us, and I must have picked the card up there. How funny it was that I had never come across it again until now.

Making some inquiries, I soon discovered that the owner of the card, Lynda, was a lady who ran a Spiritualist church in a different part of the country. It had only been a few months since I'd been to see Mary, but surely one more reading wouldn't hurt, would it?

Giving Lynda just my first name, and no further details, we arranged to meet at her home a week later.

I was greeted at the front door of a lovely home in the most gorgeous of locations, and as we walked through to the back of the house, I was afforded an exquisite view of the ocean. The house felt very peaceful, and Lynda came across instantly as a warm, kind and very friendly lady. We entered her reading room and sat for a few moments as Lynda said a prayer and then tuned into spirit.

Lynda "I have a lady called Rose who'd like to make herself known. She married Harold, and they had six children, but two died, one from disease and one through miscarriage. She is five generations back on your Mum's side."

Me "Unfortunately I haven't been able to get too far back on Mum's side, but I am currently researching my family tree, so I will definitely keep an eye out for Rose and Harold. Thank you."

Lynda "I also have a very gentle lady, she was gentle in her heart. She isn't long gone, about five years ago and she got very frail toward the end. She tells me that although she passed of cancer, she was also suffering from a slightly mild form of dementia at the end. She hadn't reached her 70th birthday and also tells me that she had a fall in the hospital. Does this make sense to you?"

Me " Yes, yes it does, my Mum passed a month after her 68th birthday, five and a half years ago and from cancer, and it sadly moved to the brain right at the very end. Mum was incredibly fragile, and yes she was taken into hospital a few months before she passed and fell out of the bed. She was so frail."

Lynda "She had a tough time didn't she? But she is so happy now. She is excitedly describing where she is. I don't think they are allowed to say too much, but she says that the creativity is amazing! She is telling me that the flowers are stunningly beautiful and are such vivid colours, so bright and intense, so much more than we could ever imagine. Your mother is completely well now."

Me "It does sound amazing, and it's wonderful to know that Mum is healthy again."

Lynda "Mum is telling me that she has three children."

Me "Yes, that's right, my elder sister, younger brother and myself."

Lynda "Was she one of five children? And she is giving me the name David."

Me "Yes, that's right, she had two sisters and two brothers, and a brother who passed when she was only two, so I don't suppose she really knew him, sadly. David was Mum's youngest brother, and they became very close in their adult years. It was awful for the children when Mum's mother passed because her father couldn't cope and the family was split. The brothers went into a children's home while Mum and her sisters were taken in by family friends. It must have been an unbearable childhood for them."

Lynda "That is very sad, but Mum wants to let you know that she is still here and that there is no need to worry. She says it's very peaceful where she is and that she went through a time of waiting while she accepted what was happening. Mum didn't want to hang on too long and to cause any trouble."

Me "Good, yes I get the feeling that she is very keen to tell us that she is still here, this isn't the first time she's said as much! I find it sad that she didn't want to cause any trouble. She had a disagreement towards the end of her life. I hope this isn't about that?"

Lynda "She is asking you not to worry about what happened at the end and adds that she wasn't quite ready to go in some ways. Don't worry, she can now see that it was the perfect time for her to leave and that everything is as it should be, so please know that she's happy now."

Me "Thank you, that's a huge relief!"

Lynda "I have just asked her what you do, and she has given me quite an old fashioned word, she tells me that you are a telephonist."

Me (laughing) "I haven't heard that word for years, how funny! Yes, I have had a couple of jobs where I worked mostly on the phone, and I am currently training to become a telephone counsellor which is 90 per cent taking calls and counselling people over the phone, that's brilliant."

Lynda "They are telling me that you are an excellent counsellor and that you'd also make a really great nurse too."

Me "Thank you, both appeal to me actually."

Lynda "Your Granddad, has stepped in, he's about 5'7/ 5'8 and is talking about your son. He is lovely and is doing some great work, Granddad tells me he manipulates colour to heal animals."

Me "Really? That sounds amazing, that's so lovely."

Lynda "He loves animals. Your son has stepped in and is asking me to tell you not to blame yourself, he says *"It wasn't your fault, Mum, I was here for the perfect amount of time, please don't worry. Please know that you did nothing wrong. I love you, Mum."*

Me (feeling incredibly emotional) "I love you too sweetheart."

Lynda "Are you a healer Lorraine?"

Me " No. No, I'm not."

Lynda "Well you certainly could be, have you ever tried carrying out Reiki? You have such strong healing energy in your hands and into your arms."

Me (shocked)"Really? I have never tried any healing I don't think I'd be very good..."

Lynda "You need to have more self-belief. I think you would be an excellent healer. I think you're blocking it for some reason, don't be afraid of your natural gifts."

Me "Thank you."

Lynda "Your son is showing me a dog, and piles of laundry, he is showing me the dog grabbing the laundry and pulling it around, she's very boisterous, and there's a lot of mess in the room, he says you won't be pleased!"

Me "Ha-ha! Yes, our dog Tilly is seven, but she still thinks she's a puppy, her bed is in the laundry room, and this is the third one we've given her as she chewed the first two. My daughter also gave her a pillow which she pulled apart, and there was stuffing everywhere. He's right, it was a real mess, and I wasn't pleased with our dog at all!"

Lynda "Oh dear, he loves the dog, though. He says that he has watched his sisters grow up and that they are all darlings. Have you lived in a house where the staircase overlooks the lounge where they played? He is telling me that he used to sit on the stairs and look through to the lounge."

Me "He has mentioned our dog Tilly, a few times now, I'm really pleased that he's fond of her. She is a lovely dog. Regarding the staircase, yes! In our first house, the bannisters had a wide gap between the wooden panels, and it was possible to sit and see through to the lounge. In our second house, and the girls would still have been young there also, we had the same arrangement but with slightly less gap between the wooden sides. You could easily position yourself to look through them, though, that's so lovely oh and we had a small playroom with all the toys in which was the room closest to the stairs in that house."

Lynda "I am asking him to tell me what your favourite food is and he is telling me that it's pasta. I"m not sure though? Is that right?"

This is the question that I covered in an earlier chapter. If you recall, I was a little mystified as to why pasta would have been selected when I have many other food preferences that I would have placed higher. It took a few moments to realise that my son was describing the scene in my kitchen the previous night when I'd attempted (and failed!) to get creative with spaghetti. Moving swiftly on from this revelation...

Lynda (laughing) "I'm afraid they give all the secrets away."

Me "Oh no, I wonder what he's going to come out with next!"

Lynda "I have just asked him to show me something you've been doing."

At this point in the reading, Lynda had turned away from me slightly and was having a mini conversation with my son. I must admit that I found it quite amusing and it went like this - Lynda "Are you sure? Really? I mean I could say that but, do you want me to, so you'd like me to? Yes, ok then."

Turning once again to face me, Lynda rather apologetically explained that she'd been asked to present some information to me, that it might seem a little strange but that she would tell me anyway.

Lynda "He is showing me that you are standing by the ocean looking out to sea and here is the strange bit, he is showing me that you are looking at a ship, and here is the funny part, it's the Titanic!"

As Lynda's words sank in, she continued to apologise and asked how I could possibly have been looking at the Titanic in Auckland, New Zealand in the year 2014. I eventually came to my senses and just about managed to string a few words together as best I could, considering the shock and complete astonishment that I was feeling!

Me "Oh my, that is just so unbelievable! I wasn't on the beach looking at the Titanic, but I was sitting at home looking at a photograph of the Titanic. My great-grandfather worked on the docks in Belfast, Ireland, where the ship was built.

I have been researching that side of my family tree this week, and only a couple of days ago, I placed the photo into a folder. Yes, you could say that I was looking out to sea as the photograph shows the ship on the ocean. That is just so amazing. I'm speechless!"

Lynda "I'm really pleased that I gave you the information now."

Me "Me too, that's brilliant. Thank you."

Lynda "He likes the garden area you have created for him."

Me "That's great to know, I had best keep up with the weeding then! I planted a white rose bush for him and have a small statue of an angel, some ceramic butterflies and a large stone with his initial on in the garden. I can see this section from my bedroom window."

Lynda "He says it looks lovely. Right, he's showing me something else, and this is also a bit odd, well the thing itself isn't strange, but it's not a very exciting image. Shall I give it to you anyway? I feel I should after the last piece of information. Yes, he's asking me to tell and to show you."

Me (excitedly) "Oh yes please."

Lynda "Ok, so he's showing me that you are, well I say it's you, but I can't see your face, but I can see your dark hair. I think it's you. So, he's showing me that you have a shoe in your hand, it's a lovely shiny shoe, and that you are sitting down and putting the shoe on and it has a strap, and you are pulling the strap into a buckle across your foot like this."

As I sat, utterly mesmerised for the second time in the space of not more than ten minutes, Lynda carried out precisely the same action as Mary had done just a few months earlier. The two women's actions were astonishingly identical! It was overwhelming, and I was, in an instant, well and truly rooted to the spot.

The goose bumps running up and down my spine were forceful and persistent, my jaw must have hit the ground! I was utterly shocked to the core. Had I actually just experienced this? Was I in some kind of a dream? No, I was definitely not dreaming, and I had most certainly not imagined what had just occurred in front of my eyes. I was irrevocably dumbfounded!

No words found their way from my lips at this time, I just sat in silence. Two completely independent, disconnected people had described, in just the same way, using the exact same actions, an everyday occurrence that at any other time would have seemed very run of the mill and somewhat boring, to prove to me, beyond all doubt, the existence of the afterlife.

My sweet mother who before her passing had laughed at and dismissed any suggestion of spirit communication. This non-believer who even revealed considerable annoyance at such charlatans, parading as mediums who prayed on the weak and vulnerable. A once fully fledged sceptic had managed to orchestrate the suggestion and delivery of a fond memory that would without question, instantaneously grab my attention.

Even more amazingly, my mother had managed to convey this astonishing masterpiece twice! Had my son also assisted her I wondered?

I was utterly speechless until Lynda's caring words broke me from my spell.

Lynda "Sorry, I did say that it was a rather dull image."

Me (frantically trying to form a semi-intelligible response) "I err, I mean, what I should say is that it well, it made perfect sense to me, thank you."

Lynda smiled, and a look of relief came over her face. We concluded the reading shortly afterwards once Lynda had delivered a final message from my son reiterating once again that his passing was of his own choosing and reassuring me once more that I did absolutely nothing wrong which I was incredibly grateful to hear. My concentration by now had disintegrated into a pulp, and I needed some time and space to process the information and image that I had just witnessed.

After thanking this talented lady for her time and energy, I climbed into my car and tried my best to ground myself.

Driving on a little from Lynda's house, I discovered a small beach, so I parked up and walked down onto the sand.

The tide was coming in, and I removed my shoes and headed into the water for a paddle.

As the waves lapped gently at my feet, I marvelled at the sight of the infinite ocean before me and thanked my loved ones for once again coming through and proving to me that they live on and are never more than a breath away. Just as my loved ones are close by, yours are too. The beautiful relationship you shared with your baby continues. The feeling of separation between life and the afterlife is nothing more than an illusion.

I pondered the correlation between my son and mother for a moment. Each of them had reached through the veil to reassure me that they will never leave. Both had consistently reinforced our eternal connection. The bond between mother and child is a phenomenal one!

As I closed my eyes for a while and fell completely into the moment, it felt as if I could reach out and embrace, *all that is - but appears not to be*. It was an amazing feeling and one that I shall never forget.

Chapter Seventeen

SENSING SPIRIT

You'll see it when you believe it

- Wayne Dyer

Several months after my reading with Lynda, I sat and reflected on all of the fantastic information that had been shared with me. I felt unbelievably blessed to have been given such unquestionably accurate evidence. I am so very grateful to each of the mediums and of course to my beautiful family members in spirit, for taking the time to connect.

I have certainly had some wonderful messages, and each reading further strengthens my belief in the continuation of life after death. I am not sure if this unwavering faith has helped me to become somehow more open to recognising and receiving signs, but I thought I would share with you some of the events that have taken place over the past few years. Perhaps you may have encountered similar goings on also.

Music has always been a vital medium to me. I love

music and almost every genre of it. I am constantly listening to songs on the radio, songs from my CD collection and yes, songs online. For me, music contains memories and meaning and literally speaks to my soul.

I have specific songs for each of my passed over family members and there are three which correlate to my son for various reasons. One of which, an oldie now from the 1980's, played on the radio, immediately after I arrived home from the very first reading he'd come through to me in. I had been living in New Zealand for seven years at this point and had never heard it played once in all of that time. Guess which song then followed me around for the next few days? It was uncanny, whichever radio station I tuned into, no matter where I was, what time of the day it was, this particular song found its way to me.

I have also experienced this with songs I know that my Mum loved, or songs that we once discussed and enjoyed together. If you too have experienced these musical signs, feel reassured that it is your loved one letting you know that they are right there with you.

Sensing that our loved ones are with us is an often ignored experience that we might quickly put down to 'imagining things' I know that I have been guilty of doing this many times and have passed off seeing something moving or appearing in the corner of my eye as just wanting something to be there.

On several occasions, I have been in deep thought about

my son, embracing all of the emotions associated with him. The incredible love and joy, the heartbreak and longing, only to experience the most powerful, intense goosebumps running not only up and down my spine but up and down and into my legs as well! They come from nowhere, last for a couple of minutes, which is just long enough to allow me to accept that they are not due to some medical or sciatic nerve problem or similar. I feel completely safe, there is no pain or discomfort, but just an unshakeable feeling that I cannot explain and most definitely cannot deny! This only ever happens when I am thinking about my son, and I'm certain that it is his way of connecting directly with me.

Feathers are often used by spirit to attract our attention. I have lost count of the many times a feather has appeared in the house coming seemingly from nowhere. I now have a small jar filled with the little white treasures and always remember to thank my loved ones for their little gifts. Coins are another item that those in the spirit world like to leave for us too.

Butterflies and birds are common signs. Robins are said to appear to remind us of our lost loved ones, but if you have another breed of bird that continues to pay you visits, the same meaning applies. It is spirit saying Hello. Butterflies are notoriously referred to as visitors from heaven, and I read that white butterflies are little ones returning to see us, which I find really lovely.

Inhaling the scent of a familiar perfume or a favourite flower can signify a visit as could the odour of cigarette or cigar smoke or the smell of a favourite type of food that your loved one enjoyed.

Perhaps you might feel a light touch or sense that somebody is there with you or maybe you detect a strange and unfamiliar sound that draws your attention to something not being quite right.

Sometimes spirit use electricity to attract our attention, for example, they may make a light/lights flicker or an electrical device switch itself on or off. Light bulbs blowing can be another form of contact.

Moving objects is another way spirit show us that they are around. An object may disappear and then reappear in a completely different place, or there may be a subtle repositioning of it, in the case of a photograph moving slightly, even though it hasn't been touched.

Number plates and street signs are also often used to remind us of our loved ones. I have on several occasions, pulled up at a set of traffic lights only to read the plate of the car in front of me or to the side and seeing a name or number relating to one of my spirit family members.

Cupboard doors or drawers opening or doors shaking are further signs from spirit.

My eldest daughter and I had a rather bizarre experience one afternoon when our double lounge doors started shaking randomly. The shaking only lasted for a couple of minutes, but it was long enough for us both to comment on the spooky happening. Desperately trying to find a logical explanation, we researched to see if the area had experienced an earthquake or similar, but nothing was noted in New Zealand for that day. There was no wind or draft, and we were the only ones in the house at the time.

While driving to an energy healing one sunny Tuesday morning, I looked up at the beautiful blue sky above and noticed that it was entirely clear, except for one enormous white cloud that had formed into a well-defined and perfectly shaped feather. It literally filled most of the sky, and I let out a small gasp as I surveyed its stunning appearance. The feather cloud remained still and didn't change shape at all for the entire length of my journey. I really wanted to photograph it, but driving at 90 km's on the motorway for a meeting that I was already running slightly late for meant that it would have been terribly unpractical. I took it as a clear sign, which the healer I was meeting up with, confirmed during my appointment.

A few evenings beforehand, I was in bed, wide awake, pondering the day's activities and generally trying to put the world to rights in a one-way conversation with myself when, suddenly, in the dark of the night, I spotted a bright light moving from one side of the room to the other. At first, it moved slowly, but then, perhaps realising that my attention had been caught, shot across the room and my eyes struggled to keep up with its rapid pace. I hadn't had time to process what was happening when the light disappeared as quickly as it had arrived.

I raised my head for a moment just making sure that there was no light source coming from outside or from somewhere inside the room, but could find no explanation. As I lay my head back onto the pillow, the strangest thing happened. I found myself staring, wide-eyed, at an enormous pair of legs! In fact, looking back, it was more comparable to a projection of a pair of very long legs, and I seemed to be viewing this projected image, which then resulted in the limbs taking a huge stride across my bed!

The legs were covered by a pair of trousers, which were made of an unusual material. The clothing didn't look like the average man made type, and I could see no higher than the waist and no lower than the ankles, but the height of the image almost filled the space before me, from the ceiling to the level of my bed. I wasn't frightened, I didn't actually feel anything at the time, and was just so engrossed in watching this random pair of limbs! Once they had crossed the bed, everything went back to normal again.

I looked over at my husband who was in a deep sleep and then lay awake for a while wondering what on earth I had just experienced, and of all the things to see, why a pair of legs? It was certainly very odd, and I knew, without a doubt, that I hadn't been dreaming.

When I recounted my experience, I was very surprised

but reassured to learn that one of my spirit guides is a Native American Indian man who has been working with me for some time. Everything fell instantly into place, the gigantic white feather in the sky that practically led me all the way to the session and the enormous legs. There was no way I was going to be able to ignore these signs!

As I sat, an image of the trouser covered legs popped into my head, and I realised that the strange looking material I couldn't place previously, was, in fact, an animal skin. Later that day, I searched online for Native American Indian clothing and found 'my legs' on a picture of a man wearing Buckskin trousers.

I have encountered many occasions where something hasn't felt quite right, and I have been forced to stop and evaluate the situation. I am not sure if these warnings are coming from Spirit or if it is simply my intuition being fired up. Unfortunately, I don't always heed the advice given, but I thought I would share with you a couple of instances where celestial insight saved the day.

Our gorgeous twelve-year-old tabby cat, Charlie, returned home from one of his daily adventures sporting a large lump on his side. He didn't appear to be in any pain, so I decided to monitor him for a while before taking him to see the vet. I certainly didn't feel as if there was any urgency and was sure that it was nothing sinister. A week later the lump was still present, and I felt that it should be looked at in case any treatment was necessary.

The following morning, having spent twenty long,

arduous minutes coaxing an extremely reluctant patient into his cat carrier, Charlie and I made our way to the local rural vet's practice. The sound of pitiful meowing filled the car from start to journey's end, and it was a relief to finally set him free inside the examination room!

As the vet palpated the lump, he remarked that it was very large. His tone changed slightly as he suggested that it didn't feel good. "It's a nasty I'm afraid. It needs to come out, and he will probably also need chemotherapy and drugs."

I stood, in utter shock, completely glued to the spot. The smell of antiseptic solution permeated the air of the cold, stark room, and I felt absolutely stunned and sick to my stomach. This diagnosis couldn't have been further from my mind. I was certain that it wasn't a tumour, but this medical expert was telling me quite unequivocally that it was.

He went on to relay a rough (extremely expensive) costing and ushered me back into the waiting room before suggesting I make an appointment for the following day. "Let's get this out as soon as possible" he proposed, before darting back into his room.

I was still reeling from the shock, but as I slowly made my way to the reception desk, something, or somebody, I'm not quite sure which, stopped me in my tracks. Something wasn't right, it was completely off, in fact, and I needed to process this intense feeling. "I'll call you to make the appointment when I'm home" I found myself mumbling and rushed out of the surgery as fast as my weak, wobbly legs would carry me!

I have no medical training and would never presume to be more knowledgeable than a fully qualified professional, yet something felt completely alien with the vet's findings. Perhaps I was in denial, after all, the facts certainly pointed towards a tumour. The overwhelming sense that something was completely amiss would not leave me, however.

Twenty-four hours later, Charlie was examined by a vet at a second practice. I felt much more at ease entering this building, it had a relaxing, comforting vibe that the other one lacked.

Following a thorough examination, by a reassuring and very pleasant professional, Charlie was diagnosed with a completely harmless cyst! I asked if it could possibly be something more concerning and was told that the lump was entirely the wrong shape and in an uncommon place.

To reassure me further, the vet drew some very ordinary looking fluid from the lump. I then shared with him, the initial vet's findings and his fee for surgery and was told in no uncertain terms that the figure quoted was almost double what it should have been.

I will never know if the first vet, after operating on our boy, would have revealed the great news or if he had other more profitable ideas in mind. It really doesn't bear thinking about. But I am so thankful that something led me to question the facts presented to me, and that I sought a second opinion.

Our furry feline friend is now approaching his fourteenth birthday and has been cyst and problem free ever since.

A second incident, in which following my intuition paid

off, occurred in 2011. I had been to see a specialist a year previously and was told that my concerns were unfounded. When the problem had still not diminished some months later, I approached a second professional who also reassured me that I had absolutely nothing to worry about.

I was a little perplexed after this appointment because I was sure that something was wrong. Resigning myself to the fact that these people were the experts, I pushed my fears aside and carried on as normal.

A year later, the niggling feeling still remained at the back of my mind, and I decided to seek advice from a third specialist. Once again, it was suggested that all was perfectly well, but he agreed to carry out some investigations, given my past medical history.

Within the week my concerns were realised, and I was scheduled to have surgery five days later!

While I would never advise a person to go against medical advice, which could, of course, be dangerously detrimental. I would say that if you have a strong gut feeling that something is wrong, do speak up.

I do not like making a fuss and completely shy away from confrontation, but I knew that something was amiss, and something (or somebody?) was not going to let me rest until I had got to the bottom of the problem. I'm so pleased that I listened.

Not all readers are created equal

I guess it was bound to happen at some point in time, after all, I had been immensely lucky with the mediums and clairvoyants that I had selected thus far. Perhaps I was getting a little too blasé about hearing from my nearest and dearest in spirit, and maybe this was their way of telling me that I needed to take a break from seeking heavenly Hellos!

Because I had now seen virtually all of the most popular mediums in Auckland, (and this surely should have been caution enough that I was perhaps getting a little carried away with my new 'hobby,') the search for a new one was proving rather fruitless. Eventually, however, I came across a lady who looked good on paper, but sadly didn't quite live up to her (few) positive testimonials. She may, of course, have just been having an off day, but our meeting was the first in which I had left feeling worse than when I went in.

The appointment got off to a rather unprofessional start with me arriving before the reader. The lady in question, who I shall refer to as 'Carolyn' rents a room in a private health practice. I entered the building with five minutes to spare before my appointment time and waited, and waited.

Fifteen minutes past the allotted time, in rushed a very flustered lady who apologised for being late and led me into a side room. We then spent a further ten minutes discussing the state of the traffic and covered some general chit chat. I felt like asking her to take a deep breath and to calm herself, it was an uncomfortable introduction and, unlike the other professionals I'd encountered, Carolyn did little to put me at ease, and I found myself feeling more than a little tense.

Carolyn then invited Spirit to come forward, and we waited in silence for a few minutes. To be perfectly honest, if I were in spirit, I'm not sure that this lady would be my favourite first port of contact, so I wouldn't have blamed them at all for deciding that they were not going to come through to her.

Thankfully my lovely Mum was not deterred and was soon talking about my family members. The lady asked me if I knew that one particular relative was going through a severe bout of depression. Yes, I confirmed that this was indeed the case and then the conversation moved onto my children. Carolyn asked how many I have, to which I said four (hoping that she would correct me) and she began describing each of my daughter's characters and personalities. I will say that she was pretty accurate and therefore, her clairvoyance skills were good.

She also told me that I would be travelling to Australia with my husband and daughters sometime within the following year (this proved to be incorrect.) Carolyn predicted that I would be going further overseas in 2016 or 2017 (this is in the planning stages right now, so yes, this information is correct)

The lady also described my husband's personality and my own quite well. The descriptions were all reasonably good, but aside from revealing that she could read energy, offered no real value in terms of discovering something that I didn't already know! (I did wonder if perhaps the reason that I had been drawn to this reader might have simply been to alert me to my depressed relation, so I made contact later that day, but thankfully all was well with them.)

All too soon, the session came to an abrupt end, before the hour was up in fact, and when I asked if my son was around, it was revealed that he hadn't wanted to come forward with a message today. I suspected that actually, he hadn't wanted to come through to Carolyn but said nothing and handed over my money.

As I have said before, perhaps the lady was just having a bad day, but I certainly learnt a valuable lesson through that rather strained session, and it is that not all readers are created equal! So, wherever possible, always choose somebody with proven credentials. Suffice to say that I shall not be recommending this lady to anybody.

Reflections

The reading with Carolyn had left me feeling rather flat and somewhat disheartened. I felt entirely reticent about booking any further readings with new mediums, resigning myself to the fact that perhaps it might be best to take a break and then to revisit one of the gifted ladies I'd previously met with, sometime in the future. I reluctantly assured myself that this was for the best and tried to busy my mind with other projects and activities.

Thankfully, I continued to feel the presence of my son

around me, and my collection of white feathers, materialising from out of nowhere, continued to grow. Still, however, I longed for the verbal connection, that only the mediums had been able to bring forth for me. I did worry that I was too needy, that I had become far too consumed with the desire for such frequent reassurances, but at the same time, if the amazing spirits were still happy to communicate and to pass on such beautiful validating messages, then had it actually become a problem?

I realise that some people might consider my interest and fascination a little intense or even unhealthy. I admit that I was pretty absorbed and in some ways, perhaps even a little addicted to visiting mediums and clairvoyants, in the year following my son's first appearance, but I was still functioning fully and continuing to lead my life as normal. I wasn't driving myself into financial difficulties or debt (thanks to birthday and Christmas present gifts of cash,) and the readings were not controlling my life - they were just adding to it.

I have spent most of my life worrying about what other people think, and it has held me back in so many ways. I decided there and then that I would no longer allow myself to listen to the disapproving murmurs of those who disagreed with my spiritual choices. I still have to bite my tongue around certain individuals, but I will not dumb down or pretend that I have not been forever changed by my awe-inspiring spiritual encounters and subsequent awakening.

Thankfully a new earth angel was about to enter my

life, who would give further credence to my ever expanding spiritual understanding. The angel in question is the genuinely gifted Juelle who I have mentioned before, and I have no doubt whatsoever that I was destined to meet this fabulously talented spiritual teacher.

My Friend Margie and I first met back in 2012 while participating in a counselling course. We were placed in a group with young twenty and thirty-somethings from various backgrounds. Some members of the group were studying Psychology at University, others were professionals adding to or updating their skills. As the only mothers in the group, we instantly gravitated towards each other and, over the months, discovered that we shared a lot in common. Our children were similar ages, and we had encountered some almost identical life experiences. Our friendship blossomed, and we met for regular coffee catch ups outside of the course. The conversation between us flowed effortlessly, and we jokingly referred to ourselves as soul sisters.

It wasn't long before we opened up further about our spiritual beliefs and Margie also revealed that she had been visiting an inspiring lady, who was an energy healer and naturopath, but also had psychic abilities passed down from her mother. Margie was certainly extremely impressed with the energy healing she'd received, and knowing that I struggled terribly at times with the loss of my son, suggested that I too book a session with Juelle.

I am not the greatest at welcoming new opportunities or jumping straight into something with both feet, and often need a little time to get used to an idea. I was also feeling a little apprehensive about the prospect of lying on a therapy table, feeling mentally exposed and overwhelmingly vulnerable as a complete stranger lay her hands on (or very close at least) to me! I agreed to take the lady's number and stored it on my phone.

Later that day, I undertook some research into the healing modalities and was surprised to learn just how many are available, from Reiki to Emotional Freedom Techniques to Theta Healing and many more in between. I firmly believe that emotional blockages can often manifest in physical symptoms and would encourage anybody contemplating having some form of energetic healing to give it a try. Research the many forms out there and see which one most appeals to you.

A couple of months passed and I had almost forgotten about the energy lady, that is until Margie came bouncing into the course meeting room one morning, beaming radiantly and telling me that she had met with Juelle a few days before and had the most amazing session ever! Her enthusiasm was contagious, and as the details of the healing became more and more evident, I knew that I had to visit this lady - and very soon!

Chapter Eighteen

ENERGY HEALING AND PAST LIFE REGRESSION

I have loved you for a thousand years, I'll love you for a thousand more

– Christina Perri

My appointment took place two weeks later. Inhaling deeply as I entered the main door of the practice, I felt a real mixture of emotions, anxiety being the most prominent. I was so completely unsure of what to expect, and felt like I had taken a giant leap outside of my comfort zone! There was no time to back out however as a very friendly looking lady was fast approaching me.

Juelle introduced herself quietly and calmly and instantly made me feel comfortable in her presence. We made our way into her office and sat and chatted for absolutely ages before I was invited to lay on the healing table. Juelle then offered to cover me with a blanket and explained that she would hold her hands some distance away from me which I found very reassuring. I relaxed a little more and tried to quieten the myriad of thoughts whirling around in my head.

As I struggled to contain my brain, Juelle explained that she would work on my chakra system and continued to tell me that there are seven energy centres in our bodies, which help to regulate all bodily processes, including our immune systems, emotions and organ function. If a chakra becomes blocked, we can feel drained in that area, and the blockage can lead to illness. Ideally, all should flow freely for optimum health and wellbeing. The seven centres are as follow:

1. **The Root Chakra** - This represents our foundation and the feeling of being grounded and safe.

Location - It is located at the base of the spine, in the tailbone area.

What affects our Root Chakra? - Survival issues such as financial independence and food.

Colour – Red.

Healing Foods - Red coloured foods like red capsicum. Spicy foods such as red cayenne peppers, Tabasco sauce and root vegetables.

2. **The Sacral Chakra** - This represents our connection and ability to accept others and to open ourselves to new experiences, sexuality and creativity.

Location - The lower abdomen (about two inches below the navel)

What affects our Sacral Chakra? - Our sense of well-being, sexuality and pleasure.

Colour – Orange.

Healing Foods - Orange coloured foods such as oranges, mandarins, mango, honey, nuts.

3. **The Solar Plexus Chakra** - This represents our ability to be confident and to be in control of our lives. Our sense of power.

Location - The upper abdomen, in the stomach area.

What affects our Solar Plexus Chakra? - Self-esteem, self-confidence.

Colour – Yellow.

Healing Foods - Yellow coloured foods including bananas, Teas like chamomile and peppermint.

4. **The Heart Chakra** - This affects our ability to love, the quality of our love past, present and future.

Location - Centre of the chest, just above the heart.

What affects our Heart Chakra? - Love, inner peace and joy.

Colour – Green.

Healing Foods - Green coloured foods like green vegetables, green fruit and green tea.

5. **The Throat Chakra** - This represents our ability to communicate, to speak our truth. Expression.

Location – Throat.

What affects our Throat Chakra? - Communication, speaking the truth, holding secrets, self-expression.

Colour – Blue.

Healing Foods - Fruits, especially those that grow on trees. Teas such as blue chamomile, natural fruit juices and clear fluids.

6. **The Third Eye Chakra** - This represents our ability to focus on and to see the whole picture. Intuition, Extrasensory perception.

Location - The forehead, between the eyes.

What affects our Third Eye Chakra? - Intuition, wisdom and imagination, the ability to think and to make decisions.

Colour – Purple.

Healing Foods - Purple coloured fruits such as blueberries, blackberries and boysenberries. Lavender flavoured tea or spices.

7. **The Crown Chakra** - This represents our ability to be fully connected spiritually. Transcendence.

Location - The very top of the head.

What affects our Crown Chakra? - Our connection to spirituality, inner and outer beauty.

Colour – Violet.

Healing Foods – Because the Crown Chakra is connected to spirituality there are no healing foods, but activities such as meditation, fresh air and relaxation are all healing. Detoxing and gentle fasts can also be beneficial.

As Juelle moved slowly around the table, I felt myself relaxing further and visualised some beautiful scenery. I then saw some vivid pictures of a glowing sunset, a rose, a forest of trees, the images kept coming, and I wondered if this was what happened during meditation or if it was characteristically connected to the healing. I certainly needed to devote some time to try this out at home.

Once the healing had finished, Juelle asked me to take my time in getting off the table and to join her once again in our seats. As I sat down, I noticed that she was adding various colours to a sketch of the outline of a body. It was explained that certain colours relate to emotions such as optimism and jealousy. Before the healing work began, we discussed my childhood and some of the challenges I'd experienced while growing up.

Juelle explained that some of the emotions relating to those difficulties were expressing themselves in the healing, she also reassured me that this was a positive thing as it meant that the negative emotions were being released. This would, in turn, improve the function of the particular chakra connected to that feeling and that I would, of course, benefit emotionally, spiritually and physically from the outpouring. I was also told that this release could continue over the next week or couple of weeks even. I certainly felt extremely relaxed and unbelievably calm. I had gained a lot from my first introduction to healing, but the benefits didn't stop there.

"Are you open to the concept of life after death and spirit communication?" Juelle asked.

I fought back the inclination to call out a loud and enthusiastic *"Am I? You bet I am!"* And instead, offered a calmer, "Yes I am", and here follows the conversation which took place that morning:

Juelle "My mother was a medium, and I'm also able to see. If you don't mind me going down this path, I have some messages for you."

Me "I don't mind at all, I'm really interested and have had a few readings before so I won't be frightened or anything."

Juelle "Great. I don't get to use the mediumship for many clients. Firstly, I must say that as you were laying on the table, I saw you laying on a bed of crystals, and I am pretty sure that this is from a past life, and in that life, you were doing what I do. I think the power frightened you, though. I think maybe you were punished, and you have brought the fear of using it again into this lifetime with you which is a great shame. Also, there are many spirits around you, and your mother is here and wants to apologise for certain things that happened in the past. She is very sorry."

At this point, Juelle continued to share some of the events, and she was spot on with her recount of the past.

Me "Thank you, there were some really hard times, but I know that Mum was only doing the best that she could with the tools she had, and she suffered terribly with anxiety and depression at times."

Juelle "She is showing me that she has a black dog with her, it looks like a Labrador."

Me "Yes, that was our family dog, Jamie, he was a very active bouncy dog. Mum loved dogs."

Juelle "He's with your mum. She just wants to let you know that she is truly sorry and that she can see things much more clearly now and knows that you weren't always treated right or listened to when you should have been, she loves you very much."

Me "It's alright, I understand that Mum was doing her best without any experience of her own to draw from and that she was struggling herself. I do forgive her and love her too, she was a great Nanny to my girls, and we shared some lovely long chats, and once I'd moved to Auckland, we'd talk for hours at a time."

We then discussed the past life Juelle had seen, and suddenly I was reminded of a past life reading I'd had several years ago, long before my son had made himself known. I had completely forgotten about it and decided to hunt for the recording once home. Hopefully, it would still be where I left it, saved with my old emails. I just hoped it hadn't been deleted!

Sure enough, my search proved fruitful, and I found it stored as an MP three recording, from back in 2010. I listened to the hour long session and was amazed to hear that a lot of the information related directly to my more recent readings. For example, the medium conducting the distance reading (I wasn't present at the time it took place, but the lady tuned into my energy) correctly confirmed that I had moved overseas and that I had one brother and one sister, amongst other information. She also sensed but was not being shown, a baby, who she felt was a boy and went on to make a remark about this being very unusual as she usually saw children easily, but was not being 'allowed' to see this baby boy.

As I listened to her slight bewilderment, the penny dropped, was she referring to my son Kieran? The following words confirmed the answer to my question. "I'm just not being shown this little boy, and I have to ask, have you suffered a miscarriage?" As you can imagine, I was rather taken aback, and a little annoyed with myself for not remembering this part of the reading and connecting the dots sooner!

I suppose if I had jotted down the details of the reading as I had with all of the others, the miscarriage and baby boy comments would have stood out like a sore thumb. Because the reading was recorded, I must have listened to it a few times five years previously and then filed and forgotten all about it.

The past life part of the recording also confirmed what Juelle had said earlier in the day. Apparently, I was a woman in Pagan times, living in Ireland, clothed in a cream cloak with a hood, which loosely resembled a Nun's outfit, but not the traditional black robes worn by modern day Nuns. The images of a St Brigid's cross and a Catholic cross were shown to the medium, which she felt suggested that this was at the time of the Druids, just as Christianity was being introduced. At a time when the two were being melded together.

In this lifetime, I was a healer who directed healing energy into people to clear them of their ailments. I also wrote philosophies and prophecies alongside healing spells and rituals, which were recorded on coarse, uneven handmade paper which was then bound with something that looked like twine. The outer covers were leather hide and were made by the local blacksmith. The brown writing produced by mixing something like clay into a paste to create a rough and ready kind of ink. What a fascinating past life. The possibility of it having taken place certainly added a further understanding to my present day fascination with Ireland and its rich history!

Two additional past lives were also revealed to me in the reading, one set in America in Victorian times, the second in more modern times, which took place in Australia. Of course, there is no way that I can say for sure that either happened. But I will certainly look at the lessons and challenges involved in both to see if there might be any unresolved emotions, phobias or remnants of either that I have brought with me into this lifetime.

There have been some impressive past life studies conducted over the years. In his book, 'Many Lives, Many Masters', Brian Weiss MD, a psychiatrist, describes his experience of treating a young patient with severe anxiety. After eighteen months of therapy, the patient, Catherine, was still suffering from recurring nightmares and panic attacks. Dr Weiss regressed her, under hypnosis, back to her early childhood years, to discover where some form of trauma might have occurred.

When Catherine was about five years old, she panicked when somebody had tried to push her off a diving board into

a swimming pool. Since then, Catherine had been afraid
of water. However, even before this incident took place,
she'd had an unexplainable fear of being in the water. Other
recollections came to light, her father's absenteeism, his
heavy drinking and occasional violent outbursts when he was
around for example. Dr Weiss worked hard with his patient
to address and to heal the issues, but Catherine made no
improvement.

During one of the therapy sessions, the Dr hypnotised
Catherine as he had done in the past. She could not recall
anything before the age of three years, so he asked her to
go deeper and to tell him about the time that her symptoms
(the deep fear of water) first arose. He became extremely
confused when Catherine began recounting a life in 1683 BC
in which she drowned in a tidal wave.

Catherine went on to describe several past lives, much
to the astonishment of the then sceptical psychiatrist. As
time passed, she went on to reveal very personal information
about Dr Weiss' son in spirit that only his very close family
members were aware of. Catherine's symptoms all became
cured after more past life regressions. Once she could see
where the root of her problems had arisen from, she was able
to heal fully.

Reassuringly, Catherine spoke of family and friends
in this lifetime, appearing in her past lives and playing
various roles. For example, a mother in one lifetime was a
sister in another and a daughter or best friend in yet another
past life. This backs up other research that I have studied,

which suggests that we generally reincarnate with the same members of our soul group in each lifetime.

The medium who performed a distance past life reading on me told me that my Mum has been my mother in many lives as well as 'playing' the part of other relatives. My husband and I shared a romantic past life together in medieval Scotland when he was a soldier, and I was his maiden.

This leads me on to the question of reincarnation in babies...

Because our little angels are souls with wisdom far greater than their earthly ages would suggest, they are able to choose each of their incarnations. Our precious little ones can also determine the length of time that they remain in each life, and also choose when they are going to come back again to be with us.

For example, I have been told that my son has decided to remain in spirit and will wait for me to join him before reincarnating again in the next lifetime, or he may opt to stay in Heaven. Another passed over baby may decide to come back to his parents once again in this lifetime, as a subsequent sibling. He may have felt that the timing wasn't right first time around, or that he wanted to re-join the family as a second, third or youngest child for example.

If you are worried that you have had no signs from your angel or if mediums are not bringing messages through for you, then the chances are that your little one is already physically with you once again. Souls can also choose which gender they wish to be, so don't be alarmed if you lost a son but have now gained a daughter or vice versa.

We have all heard the stories of child prodigies who arrive on earth and after only a few very short years demonstrate remarkable talents in a particular area of life. The three-year-old who paints amazing portrait or landscapes with the eye and skill of a much more mature artist, for instance, or the child who speaks fluently in a foreign language, having received the most minimal amount of tuition.

The Austrian composer Wolfgang Amadeus Mozart springs to mind also. At the tender age of just three years old, he began picking out chords on a harpsichord. At the age of four, he could play short pieces and began composing at five. At the grand old age of just six years, Mozart, as he later became famously known as, performed in his first public concert!

A lesser known child prodigy, Dublin-born, William Rowan Hamilton, had mastered Greek, Latin and Hebrew by the age of five. The future mathematician, born in 1805, had learnt a further ten languages by his thirteenth birthday! These included Italian, Syriac, Arabic, Sanskrit, Persian and Indian dialects.

Hamilton became a professor of astronomy at Trinity College Dublin, and Royal Astronomer of Ireland, while still at university. Ireland's most famous mathematical physicist and astronomer was knighted in 1835. He is most well-known for discovering the algebra of quaternions. A very impressive sounding accolade which sadly means very little to me but

I'm sure means a great deal to those in the know! Born the fourth child of nine, William was obviously an exceptionally gifted young man.

Were these children just exhibiting random extraordinarily rare gifts, or had they perhaps previously learnt their craft in past lives? I find this possibility completely fascinating!

Chapter Nineteen

INDICATIONS FROM AN IN-LAW

*Goodbyes are only for those who love with
their eyes. For those who love with heart and
soul, there is no such thing as separation*

- Rumi

Alongside visiting mediums by myself, I have also been
asked, on a couple of occasions, to accompany others to
readings and demonstrations. At such meetings, I usually act
as a scribe, jotting down all incoming information as quickly
as my pen allows. As I suggested earlier in the book, in the
chapter covering preparation for a reading, having one person
on hand to write everything down allows the second to
absorb the information brought forward fully and renders the
need for multi-tasking unnecessary.

Looking back through my golden book, jam packed full
of readings, I came across one encounter which amusingly
had the two of us passing the pen and notebook back and

forth as if we were playing a game of pass the parcel. It might be worth bearing in mind that if you do decide to take somebody along to a reading with you, and you are hoping for the messages to be directed only at you, a friend is probably the best person. If you decide to take a relative along for the ride, you may need to be prepared to share the limelight.

My eldest daughter had been experiencing a few unusual occurrences in her bedroom. These included seeing a book fall randomly from a shelf, despite not being touched or moved in any way, an unfamiliar, (or perhaps an unrecalled) scent that would come and go, her I-pod dock turning on and off spontaneously and several extremely vivid dreams. In view of these instances, she decided that a visit to a Spiritualist church might be in order, just in case somebody was trying to get a message across.

We searched online and found that the church with the most convenient day and time for us both, was in Ponsonby, a lovely inner city suburb situated not far from the centre of Auckland. The online information read pleasantly enough, and the only problem with this selection was that we hadn't been in the country for very long at this point. I had never been to Ponsonby before, had no GPS to guide us and had only really glanced very quickly at the map before setting off on our journey!

To cut a long story short, after many frustrated thoughts and words-and after much debate about turning the car around and heading straight back home again, we eventually arrived at our destination, at precisely the same moment that the speaker had begun climbing the steps up onto the stage! I felt as if I was back at school again, rushing late into the classroom only to be confronted with thirty odd heads and pairs of eyes suddenly turning my way, their focus fixed firmly on me and a look of sheer disdain on the teacher's face.

In reality, my panic was unwarranted as, on this occasion, nobody turned to stare, and I didn't experience the desperate, overwhelming need for the ground to open up and swallow me. There were no repercussions or mention of after school detentions, and we actually managed to sneak in quite unobtrusively, sliding silently into the seats closest to the door before the chairperson had begun her address.

The visiting medium, a jolly Scottish lady, whose name I sadly missed, began to explain that she worked by sharing accurate information from spirit, to the audience, rather than to an individual person, and that once a connection was made, the information would (usually) flow. Because of this, she asked us all to be brave and to speak up if we could accept any relevant forthcoming information.

I glanced at my daughter and pulled a worried face, as the prospect of speaking out in front of such a large gathering of people filled me with absolute dread. Judging by the expression on my daughter's face, I could instantly see that she wasn't too enamoured with the idea either. Because of this, I doubted very much that we would receive a message. I felt as if we had unleashed an unspoken block, and that members of our spirit family would sense our discomfort and not pursue the idea of making contact.

Fortunately for us, it would appear that our loved ones remain precisely the same once they enter spirit, that is to say, that their personalities and mannerisms do not change at all. My lovely, but very strong willed and direct, mother in law was most certainly not going to let a few nerves prevent her from coming through and delivering her thoughts and advice!

Medium "I have a lady who has recently passed, not very long ago at all actually, I would say in the last year, maybe more recently than this even. She is not from New Zealand, and I want to come to this area of the room."

As she spoke, the medium walked over to the side of the hall that my daughter and I were seated in and reached out her arm in our general direction. I racked my brains to place the person in spirit and was so busy trying to make things fit for my mother that I didn't fall in for a while. There was absolutely no way that I would speak up and draw attention to myself unless I was completely and utterly positive that the information was for us, so I kept quiet.

"This lady had an adult child pass before her into spirit, she lived in England or Scotland, because she is showing me that it's on the other side of the world, near where I come from. The name Gwen is very significant to her"

At this moment, I felt the strongest of goose bumps flowing up and down my spine, and immediately turned to my daughter to exclaim "I think it's Grandma!" We locked eyes for a second, each of us willing the other to speak up.

After a few seconds, I knew I had to find my voice. Besides, I had tried desperately hard not to upset my mother in law when she was alive, I daren't rock the boat now!

Me (very sheepishly raising my hand) "I think the message might be for us."

Medium "Thank you, can you accept the information I've given so far?"

Me "Yes I can, my mother in law Teresa passed eleven months ago, her daughter Angela passed when she was 25, and they lived in England. Teresa's mother's name was Gwen."

There were a couple of audible gasps in the audience, and the medium continued. "Thank you, she's showing me her teeth, and they look a bit, well, broken and she is telling me that she didn't like going to the dentist because she felt it was too expensive and didn't like to waste her money there."

My daughter and I exchanged smiles and laughter at this comment because Teresa would often complain about the extortionate prices that dentists charged and would refuse to give in to any dental procedures, no matter how bad, unless she was in absolutely excruciating pain and discomfort. This was a very prominent and well-known problem that everybody in the family was aware of and a very significant piece of information.

Medium "She is telling me that you have a picture that was hers, a picture of where she lived, and it's hanging in your house now."

I tried desperately to recollect a picture of my mother in law's house, but couldn't place the information, and must have sat there looking terribly vague, that is until my daughter nudged me and whispered "The London one!" By now, I had handed my notebook over to my daughter, and she was frantically jotting down every last word.

Me "Oh yes, I think I know what she means, she had a picture of London, a sketch really, with landmarks on, it used to hang in her dining room, I brought it back here with me, and it is hanging in my house. We all lived in London. I was thinking of a particular picture of a house."

Medium "Yes it's easy to get stuck, to think of one idea and to try to make it fit, luckily spirit won't stop until we have worked out the accurate message and this lady wasn't going to stop until you got it!"

Me (laughing) "I'm really pleased we worked that one out, I don't want to get told off!"

Medium "No you're all good! She said that she left you a soft toy."

Me "Did she? (a slight pause) Oh yes, yes of course she did, it's an elephant. She loved elephants and often brought back little wooden ones from her travels to South Africa. This one was a gift for my daughter, but she was frightened of it because it was a soft toy that would walk forward, lift its trunk and make a deafening noise!"

My Daughter "I remember that I was terrified of it!"

Medium "She is telling me that somebody is not treating you as they should, she is asking me to say that you need to speak up for yourself and that you are not to let them put you down. She's also saying that she is really pleased that the four grandchildren got the brooches she left for them."

Me "I'm not quite sure...she did have four grandchildren, though, my four daughters."

This piece of information didn't make any sense whatsoever to me at the time, but later, once home, as we recounted the gist of our meeting and read out our handwritten notes to my husband, his eyes lit up immediately on hearing this part of the communication.

Mark explained that the four rings with stones in, one left to each of our girls, were in fact made using stones from his great-grandfather's tie pins, and although the medium hadn't been 100% accurate with her interpretation, a brooch and a tie pin are very similar of course. The fact that my husband, a typically cool, unimpressed sceptic, was able to acknowledge the news, was very pleasing indeed. I did wonder if my mother in law used this snippet of information to reassure my husband because he was the only person who knew about the origin of the jewellery. It would have been so much easier for her just to have mentioned the rings! Spirit can be tenacious and brilliant when they want to be.

Medium (looking at my daughter now) "I would like to come to you now. This lady is telling me that she used to love watching you singing and dancing. Your Gran wants you to keep it up, she is telling me that you will use these skills in your career one day, she's not saying that you will necessarily be a singer or a dancer but that these things will help you to help others, does this make sense?"

My Daughter "Before coming to New Zealand, when we were living in England, I sang in a choir and also belonged to a dance and drama club. My grandma often came to watch me."

Medium "She is also telling me to ask you not to worry so much and saying try not to put so much pressure on yourself, keep working hard at school but take time for yourself, everything will be alright."

My Daughter "Ok, thank you."

Medium "I'm also hearing that you have felt like your grandmother has been with you, is that right?"

My Daughter "Yes, I have thought so, but wasn't sure."

Medium "Trust those feelings, it's alright to trust your intuition. She is telling me that she is very proud of you and sends lots of love to you, oh and you have been getting tension headaches and stiff shoulders because that's where you store stress, she wants you to drink lots of water and to relax more. Teresa sends you both and all of the family lots of love."

Both "Thank you so much."

We were delighted to have received such a fantastic confirmation that my daughter's grandmother was well and had been looking out for us all. At that time, my daughter was still studying at school and hadn't decided which career path she was going to follow. She was working incredibly hard and at times suffered from stress.

After the reading, she went on to complete her high school education, has obtained a university degree and is now working as a teacher. Music and drama are subjects that she actively encourages and brings to the classroom, alongside running vocal and dance classes for a variety of pupils.

Chapter Twenty

MAGICAL MOMENTS IN THE MOST MAGICAL OF PLACES

*May the road rise up to meet you, May the
wind always be at your back,*

*May the sun shine warm upon your face, the
rain fall soft upon your fields,*

*And until we meet again, may God hold you in
the palm of his hand.*

- Irish Blessing

I have had quite a fascination with Ireland and all things
Irish for some years as I have previously mentioned, but I
hadn't quite anticipated the deep calling which has grown
and gripped me throughout the past year. It seems almost
unbelievable that just a few years previously, I had been so
very quick to dismiss a medium's prediction that I would take
a trip to the Emerald Isle. The thought had never entered my

head, and Ireland is so incredibly far from New Zealand. I honestly thought that such a visit would be impossible and gave it no further consideration.

Little did I know that my lovely, thoughtful husband had organised a surprise break there for my 50th birthday and in September 2016, the number one experience on my bucket list was about to be ticked off.

The moment I stepped onto Irish soil, I felt instantly at peace. The experience was quite bizarre, I felt a deep sense of comfort and an overwhelming sense of having returned home, yet how could a place that I had never before been to, feel like home? I wondered if it could simply be the connection to and through my ancestors that induced such feelings of familiarity, but somehow it seemed to be much more than this.

We spent twelve wonderful days touring around Northern, Western and a little of Central Ireland. The weather, which is characteristically wet, wet, wet, all year around, behaved impeccably for us which was a relief and a blessing. We had just one day of rain and as a result were able to get out and about to explore some breathtaking places.

Perhaps, because of my relaxed holiday mode state of mind, or maybe because of the connection to the ancestors, I felt very spiritually open throughout the trip. Some people attend yoga and meditation retreats, others visit holy sites and go on pilgrimages to find themselves or to connect to a higher power. I can honestly say that simply being with Mother Nature in this most stunning of countries led to some truly magical experiences and without a doubt, fulfilled a real spiritual calling.

It is rather an old cliché to say that a place can change a person, but I honestly believe that I returned from Ireland a different person and am so grateful that I had the chance to experience my mini metamorphosis in such a lovely location.

There are so many beautiful towns, villages and stunning sights to see in and around Ireland, but there were a few that stood out for me personally and provided me with some incredible food for thought. I will share these with you now and will allow you to make up your own minds as to whether my 'homecoming' was imagined or real.

County Donegal is a gorgeous place with the most dramatic of scenery. It is situated in northwestern Ireland and borders the Atlantic Ocean. While here, we visited ancient castles, climbed mountains, explored a national park and discovered the stunning sea cliffs at Slieve League. It was here, beside the 2000 foot high, sheer rock cliffs, that I had my first reassurance that members of my family in spirit were very much with me.

As I stood, leaning over the safety rail as far as I possibly could, to gain a glimpse of the vast ocean so far beneath me, I felt rather oddly as if I were not alone.

We had very fortunately, picked a quiet day, and most of the fellow tourists were off scaling the mountains beyond the cliffs. Hubby wanted to take on the challenge also, so I watched part of his ascent then headed back over to the viewing platform, after agreeing that I would remain where I was and wait for him to join me later. I somehow felt the need to be still, to truly absorb the atmosphere, to simply 'be'.

I followed the safety railing along the cliff edge, pausing at several different points to take photos, and to admire different aspects of the scenery, then headed for a bench to sit and look through the pictures I'd captured. As I scrolled through the collection, I noticed what looked like a couple of spots, (round white bubbles I guess is the best description) on a few of the images. I didn't think too much of it but was a little surprised to see that photographs taken at previous locations were absolutely orb free.

After a short rest, I once again headed over to a different part of the area and stood close to the safety rail, resting my hands gently on it, taking in as much of the absolutely stunningly spectacular scenery as I could. Craning my neck back to observe the tips of the mist covered cliffs, I once again sensed that unmistakable feeling of being accompanied, and for some reason, found myself closing my eyes and asking my mum if she was there. I'm not sure why, but she was the one who immediately came to mind. I then opened my eyes and glanced downwards at the crashing waves beneath me.

Some moments later, removing my right hand from the rail, in preparation for a spot of cliff climbing and weary husband spotting, my attention was caught by some letters that had been scratched into the wood. How annoying that graffiti had been inflicted at such a beautiful site I thought to myself, scanning the rail for more, which thankfully was nowhere to be found. As I looked a little closer at the writing, I was extremely surprised to see that the letters formed a name- *Isobel,* which is my mother's name. I stood in awe at this incredible synchronicity!

We based our itinerary on visiting towns where relatives and more distant ancestors had lived, places that had ties to family basically. We did of course stop at random locations along the way but had pre-booked our main accommodation, at only relevant places.

For some reason, however, I felt the need to visit Galway - a town that holds no connection whatsoever to my family, and a place that I had not researched at all. Fortunately, my husband was happy to divert off course, and we arrived to sunshine and the sound of buskers whose melodic tones carried through the vibrant narrow winding streets of the central town area.

As we ambled along past a spoon player, guitarists and singers, it felt great to be in the middle of such an upbeat location. This place certainly had a fantastic vibe. We stopped momentarily to peer through the window of a brightly painted gift shop, then left the main street to explore some of the back streets, which looked just as fascinating and had retained much of their medieval history.

We had just turned the corner of a second street when I was abruptly stopped in my tracks. My head was filled with what I can only describe as a flashback, though a flashback from where I wasn't sure! I had literally been there for no more than a few seconds when this occurred, but I instantly saw the entire street in great detail, in my mind, and then recalled that I had seen it before, but in a dream! The image lasted for about a minute at most and then was gone.

I became a little frustrated with myself as, try as I might, I just could not remember anything else. It was a very short-lived incident but one that I can only describe as extremely vivid. Perhaps it had just been a case of Deja vu, but it still left me with many questions, the most pressing one of course was had I possibly been here before? The place certainly felt warm and familiar. If I had, then it most certainly hadn't been in this lifetime! Ireland was indeed beginning to awaken many mysterious phenomena's for and in me.

While we are on the topic of dreams, of which I, like most of us, have had many, I would like to share an unforgettable one that I experienced. With the exception of a few remarkable ones, they are usually just my subconscious clearing away the daily rubbish and everyday events, some are bizarre, some are just plain monotonous. I have also had one which was entirely different from any other. It was so very vivid yet simple in its form, and I suspect this was to convey the central message clearly - a no frills required type of thing.

My dream took place back in October 2008. My mother had been under the care of her local hospice for five weeks at this point. We had endured the sombre warning that Mum wasn't expected to make it through the night on several occasions throughout this period, only for this amazing lady to fight back and prove the medical staff wrong each time.

One evening, as I drifted off to sleep, I saw a stage set, I can still visualise the raw wooden posts at each side of the makeshift stage, and it was definitely a work in progress! I have never actually considered colour or the lack of it in a dream before, and I'm not sure why, but I also recall the scene before me being shown in black and white. I do not know if this was an important detail to remember but the overall simplicity and starkness of the picture struck me for some reason.

On the stage before me, were two stick figures, standing opposite each other, face to face, arms outstretched and holding hands. I somehow 'knew' that one was Mum and the other was a nurse. Suddenly, the nurse figure let go of my mother's hands, and I can recall a feeling of panic enveloping me as I shouted *"NO! DON'T LET GO!"* I then watched Mum falling gently backwards, in very slow motion. I couldn't see her again after this but somehow knew that she was ok, that she had landed softly - somewhere!

Two days later my lovely mum passed on. I like to believe that she was preparing me for her imminent departure from the earthly plane, and was letting me know it was time for her to release herself from the pain and physical struggle while reassuring me that she'd be safe. I can still recollect everything about that nocturnal vision, and I refer to it as my 'dream-plus.'

Returning to Ireland once again, I experienced a much

more pleasant dream/vision? I'm not quite sure what to call it really, but I was reminded of it while standing at the base of a hill fort once owned by one of the more compelling ancestors in my family tree.

While reading through historical books about the Emerald Isle, it soon became apparent that Brian Boru was without a doubt the most famous high king of Ireland and perhaps the greatest military leader the country has ever known. I shall now attempt to share with you an extremely shortened version of his life.

Brian Mac Cennetig was born around the year 941, in Killaloe, County Clare. His elder brother had become king following the death of their father in 951, and the two fought bravely against invading enemies, namely the Norse men.

Around 976, following the murder of his brother by the Norse, Brian became the new king of Munster and avenged his brother's death, by killing the ruler of the Norsemen in Limerick, and his sons. He fought against and defeated all rivals for the throne and went on to secure much of southern Ireland.

In 997, or thereabouts, Brian made an alliance with the reigning Ui Neill high king, Mael Sechnaill, and the pair divided the country into two divisions. Brian ruled the south, and Mael ruled the north. Around 1002, Mael surrendered the title of 'High King' to Brian.

This was a monumental achievement because Ireland at that time was bound by tradition, and political power had been dominated for the previous 500 years, by the single great dynasty-the Ui Neill. This clan of rulers were a force to be reckoned with and for half a millennium denied powerful rulers the right to take the title by using tradition and propaganda. Brian Boru flouted convention and proved that it was possible to take up the high kingship despite not being a descendant of the Ui Neill dynasty.

Brian fought well against the invading Norse warriors who imposed taxes and murdered many of his tribe. Despite having only a small army, his skill as a tactician led him to defeat much larger forces and very soon rumours began spreading that Brian possessed a vast and mighty army of men, which in turn encouraged others to join him. He was considered a hero among the Irish people for restoring the country to greatness after the invasion.

He earned his name of 'Brian of the Tributes' by collecting money from the minor rulers of Ireland and using it to rebuild ruined churches and monasteries and to construct new ones. Brian also sent overseas to replace lost artefacts and books.

This brave man practically did everything humanly possible to put right the damage that the pillaging Norse men had inflicted on his beloved country. He was considered a very generous benefactor and was an active supporter of the Irish church, who backed him, and he upheld the claim of Armagh in Ulster, to be Ireland's religious capital. He is said to have made a journey around the whole country in 1005.

Sadly, just as his Norse enemy were retreating and the war had been won, Brian was fatally wounded, on Good

Friday 1014 at the famous battle of Clontarf, a place north of Dublin. He is referred to as the last great king of Ireland and is remembered as the king who saved his people from foreign enemies, led them to victory and completely altered the course of Irish politics in the 11th century.

The Brian Boru Ring Fort stands a mile from Killaloe, overlooking the Lough Derg on the river Shannon, in Ireland's County Clare. It is set in the most stunning of places, and although it was just a half mile walk from the main road, it very much felt as if I had been suddenly transported to some secret mystical haven, far from the madding crowd!

After walking around the outside edge of this most impressive man-made structure, having admired the almost 12 foot high incredibly steep sides, I glanced up at the imposing trees that clothed the banks, their branches spilling out at amazing angles. These majestic soldiers, powerful protectors of the fort ramparts.

Scrambling up to the top of the slope, rather ungracefully I might add, I was met by the most spectacular view, through the trees, across to the Lough and Shannon River. A solitary swan glided gracefully across the water as a gentle breeze circulated around me, causing the trees to stir. I was absolutely mesmerised!

A few minutes later, I reluctantly readjusted my attention once more. Glancing down at the ditch beneath me, I observed that it was almost saucer shaped, the inside slopes falling much more gently than the outside and I carefully made my way down to the base. Standing there amidst the sound of bird song and the gentle rustling of leaves, I once again encountered the unmistakable feeling of being 'accompanied.'

As I traversed to the very centre of this ancient site, a single green leaf tumbled gently from the top of a statuesque giant, continuously circling as it made its way down from an unfathomable height, before quietly resting before me. As I crouched down to retrieve it from a bed of nature's treasures. I was instantaneously reminded of a dream or a vision perhaps, that I'd had a couple of nights previously. How could I not have remembered it before now? Maybe it was tied to my visit of this most spectacular of places?

I was standing in what can best be described as a glade, when suddenly before my eyes fell a vast sprinkling of the greenest leaves I had ever seen. Standing, transfixed, I recognised the tree from which they were cascading down, in an almost waterfall effect, but with a much slower speed and gentle fashion. The tree was an Oak, and I felt wonderfully at peace, just gazing at this astonishingly serene and soothing sight. The leaves fell quietly, and as soon as one row of greenery had touched the ground, it was instantly replaced by a second and a third and so on, producing a relentless shower that spanned across the entire section of the forest.

It was truly the most amazing, breath-taking spectacle, and every unique detail came to life in my mind as I knelt in this equally incredible space.

But what could it signify I wondered? I considered the magnificent vision for a moment longer and examined the possibility of it being in some way, a message from the ancestors. Maybe they were reiterating what I already knew to be true, thanks to the phenomenal messages from my loved ones in spirit - that life continues eternally. The circle of life - *Birth, Death and Re-Birth.*

Whatever the implications of my encounter, one thing I knew for certain, as I climbed back up the bank and out of the fort, was that I had never felt closer to my Celtic ancestors than I did at that moment. Pausing to pick a clover from the ground just outside the fort entrance, I imagined Brian Boru and his men sitting together, enjoying a hearty meal cooked on an enormous welcoming fire, the sound of laughter permeating the air. I hoped that if Brian were looking down at his amazing Beal Boru, he would be pleased to see that one of his distant great-grandchildren had made this journey to honour the greatest high king of Ireland and his story.

If you find yourself especially drawn to a particular country or place, or if you perhaps develop a real thirst for a specific culture or activity, it might be worth meditating on it gently for a while, to see if anything comes to light.(I believe that we all have the potential to tap into our intuition to gain further insight.)

Also, if you feel inclined, carrying out some research to see if you may have ancestors from this place could be a useful first step. If you have a passion for delving further into the possibility of past lives, you might like to follow a recorded meditation, specifically designed for this, or to consult a trained healer who specialises in Past Life Regression.

PART NINE

ILLUMINATION

Chapter Twenty-One

SEEING THE BIGGER PICTURE

What we have once enjoyed and deeply loved
we can never lose, for all that we love deeply
becomes a part of us

– Helen Keller

My second visit to Juelle took place a few months after the first. I had a couple of minor health niggles which I thought might benefit from a holistic approach, and given her training and experience as a naturopath, I hoped that she might be able to help.

As always, I was made to feel extremely comfortable in her presence, and we sat and chatted for over an hour, Juelle asking me various questions to decipher the best course of action. I felt totally at ease and was made to feel that we had all the time in the world, unlike a lot of my rushed visits to the GP where it was often very much a case of "Hello, yes I see, well here you go, goodbye."

We decided on a plan of action, and I felt confident that we could begin to alleviate my symptoms. I gathered that the session had concluded and started preparing to leave the room when Juelle announced that my son was with us. The conversation continued like this:

Juelle "I meditated before you arrived and your son came through then, he's actually been with us throughout, waiting patiently."

Me "That's so lovely. I honestly thought that this would be more of a medical appointment and wasn't expecting to hear from spirit at all, what a brilliant bonus!"

Juelle "Spirit like coming through for you because you have a pure spirit also, you attract them."

Me "Thank you, I love hearing from them."

Juelle "He is so close to you, all the time. His love is so strong, and he is asking me to tell you not to feel bad about anything. He is telling me you really miss that you were unable to hold him in your arms, he says that you wrestle with the pain from this deeply. The physical longing is so relentless, but he wants me to tell you that he loves you so much and that it was nothing you did wrong, nothing at all. Please don't ever think that it was."

Me "That's absolutely right. I desperately grieve for the babe in arms. The fact that I didn't get to hold him, or to kiss him, really upsets me still."

Juelle "He is so clear, he's the most connected spirit I've seen for a long time, shall I describe what I'm seeing and feeling?"

Me "Yes please."

Juelle "He is this happy, artsy, cheeky, dashing, light, angelic, ethereal looking gentle soul. He has lighter rather than darker hair, he is just gorgeous! He is talking to me about poetry. I'm not sure if he writes or if you do? He definitely has a way with words, though, he has a great sense of humour too."

Me "I do like writing poetry and recently wrote a poem for and about him. Your description, it's funny, another medium described Kieran using some of the exact same words as you did, and that is amazing, thank you!"

Juelle "You're very welcome. He's asked me to say that he feels that it would be healing for you to create. He is suggesting that you paint. He asked me not to suggest that you sketch because you'd panic and say that you can't draw."

Me (laughing) "That's so true, I can just about manage matchstick men drawings but as for anything else, well no."

Juelle "He says that he will help you to paint and that in some way, the painting will look like or somehow be about him. I think you might need to get some paint."

Me "Yes I think so too!"

Juelle "He wants me to tell you again that he decided when to leave, it was his soul's journey."

Me "Thank you."

Juelle "He chose you because of your unique qualities, he expressly wanted you, and no other. I feel like he was a gift for you."

Me "Thank you, that's so lovely. Those words you just used, this is so strange. I used those words in my poem. In two of the lines. In one I thank him for choosing me and no other, and in a separate part of the writing, I describe him as being a precious gift. That is so odd but really wonderful!"

Juelle "While he is here and strong, would you like to do a guided meditation so that you can be with him? I can hold his energy as we go."

I nodded in agreement, closed my eyes and relaxed back into the chair...

Juelle *"You are in a long hallway with doors either side of you. You walk along the hallway towards a green door*

*which is at the far end, and it is facing you. Once you get
to the door, you reach for the handle, turn it and push the
door open wide. Looking out, you can see the most beautiful
garden and a step leading down into it. You step down and
find yourself listening to the relaxing sound of birdsong in the
distance. You can smell the beautiful fragrance of flowers all
around you, and you feel the warmth of the sun as it peeps
through the treetops.*

*There is a path in front of you, and you walk along it,
admiring the green grass, the beautiful coloured flowers and
the tall and graceful trees. You can feel a gentle breeze on
your face, and you are feeling very relaxed and are enjoying
the many amazing sights around you. As you continue along
the path, you see a waterfall and a little stream. You stop to
take your shoes off and paddle in the warm water for a while.
When you are ready, you step back onto the path and notice a
bench in the distance.*

*You walk towards the bench, watching the butterflies
dancing around you as you go. As you get closer, you notice
figures standing by the bench, they are looking towards you,
welcoming you as you approach. As you get even closer, you
recognise the figures as your loved ones in spirit, they are all
smiling and waiting to greet you. You move closer to them,
and perhaps embrace them, then take a seat on the bench.
You sit with them, chatting and sharing things you wish to tell
them.*

After some time, you stand and say your goodbyes, telling

them once more the things you need to say. You hug them again and start walking slowly back along the path. As you reach the stream, you look back, and your loved ones are smiling and waving.

You continue along the path and reach the green door once again. You step up and turn the handle, pushing the door wide open. As you turn for one last time, to glance at the garden, you know that you can visit again anytime and that your loved ones will be there to meet you. Turning back towards the door, you walk inside and find yourself in the hallway. You close the green door behind you and walk along the length of the hallway back to the room you were first in. You walk to your chair and sit down. You are now acutely aware of the seat below you and slowly start wiggling your fingers and toes and bringing your awareness back into the room."

As I slowly came back into full consciousness, I felt deeply moved but amazingly relaxed. I was shocked to discover that I had tears streaming down my face and I'm not sure how long I had been releasing them, but it was long enough for my top to have collected two small pools of water, as the tears dripped down from my face. This was completely out of character for me. I have never cried in public before and am usually tremendously self-conscious and extremely wary of getting anywhere close to breaking down. Yet here I was, completely surrendering to the experience, without even realising it. It was such a powerful thing to have encountered, and it took me a while to fully process what had just occurred.

I hope that this meditation, or perhaps a similar one, can benefit others as it did me. I unequivocally felt as if my loved ones were right there with me, and I found it hugely healing and beneficial to talk to them and to say things that I'd loved to have said to them when they were alive, but couldn't. I often revisit the beautiful garden and meet up with my spirit family, and I hope that you get a chance to do the same.

I next caught up with Juelle several months later, at the end of 2015. At this time, it had been almost four years since the very first mention of my son, and it was coming up to three years since the penny had dropped and I'd finally paused and fully considered the possibility of his existence.

As with anybody grieving the loss of a loved one, some days are better than others, and the pain comes in waves that ebb and flow. On the one hand I feel overwhelmingly grateful for and amazed by, the unfolding treasures that have found their way to me over this period of time, but on the other hand, I have also felt utterly distraught at knowing that I will never get to hold my son in the physical.

Being unable to see what he looks like, and having no choice other than to accept that I will never watch him take part in everyday activities and events as his sisters have, literally consumes me with a passion and intensity that at times shocks me to my core.

Besides wrestling with these demons, I still feel very guilty because I hadn't known that I'd lost my son until many years later, and this fact has made me question my right to grieve in the same way as others. This combination of guilt and pain, when added to the difficulty of being unable to talk about my story freely and openly, further exasperates the situation!

Thankfully, in time, these feelings have started to abate. Although my pain can still be triggered by the mention of a baby boy or by the sight of a moving poem or quote describing the relationship between a mother and her son, it is now taking me slightly less time to recover from such triggers. Don't get me wrong, I cannot ever anticipate a day coming when I am not still touched in some way, and I will never stop missing my son.

Perhaps I am now entering a new phase, however, in which I am accepting my pain a little better. One in which I am learning to walk forwards, rather than backwards, while taking my beautiful boy with me. Knowing that Kieran is, and always has been, around me, albeit in spiritual form, is a colossal healing tool in itself. My hope is that in knowing your angels and loved ones are still with you, that you will never feel alone or worry that they have left because they are still very much around and always will be.

What I love most about my visits to Juelle, apart from hearing from my loved ones, of course, is that she always instinctively knows what I need from each session, even before I do! My visit to her in March 2016 was no exception.

The *why* question was one that had never really left me, why had my son not remained with me in this lifetime, did I not love him enough? Was my desire to have him not substantial enough? I found both of these concepts incredibly vexing, for hadn't I wished for my son and from such an early age too? Was my longing somehow not transmitted to him? Was I not good enough to be his mother?

These torturous questions played, and replayed regularly in my mind and left me feeling completely exasperated! Despite being told that losing him wasn't my fault, I still felt that the decision Kieran took to return home, must somehow be of my making. I was considering this relentless list of questions while driving to my appointment. Once there, I settled down on the table and began pushing all thoughts from my mind. As always, this took a little while, but eventually, I felt completely relaxed and ready to fully embrace the energy healing being given.

As Juelle worked her magic through each of my chakras, releasing negative emotions and restoring each area as she went, I felt myself relaxing further. Once I'd sensed her working through each energy system, and after she'd been moving slowly around the table for some time, I felt her pause behind me, and an incredible warmth came over my forehead and crown areas. She later explained that my third eye, which had been initially resistant to open at first, due to my fear of rediscovering my past life memories, had slowly begun opening in past sessions, and was now fully open.

I told her about some dreams and experiences that I'd had in recent months, which Juelle confirmed would have come as a result of this progress. I was then told that I would now start seeing the bigger picture.

At the time, I wasn't quite sure what this meant, but in hindsight, I now believe it meant that I would finally receive some clarity regarding my son's decision to leave his earthly incarnation early. I was then told that my son had sent Juelle an image of two unfolding Lotus flowers, and was asked to visualise my own and Kieran's hearts beating rhythmically in time with the petals as they opened and closed. I can remember feeling extraordinarily moved by this image, and at that moment, I felt remarkably connected to my son.

Juelle then proposed that I could also visualise roses if I preferred, which was an interesting comment for her to have made because I associate white roses with my son and have bought them in remembrance of him on many occasions. Kieran then asked Juelle to *remind my Mum to see the beauty in everyday things* and I, of course, agreed to make more effort to do so. The following exchange then followed:

Juelle "Kieran is showing me himself out in nature, he is out in a beautiful pasture, and if you can picture a stunning summer's day with that very high sunlight that gleams through the tops of the trees, streaming down onto the land. He is so happy and contented, and he's running through the grass so freely. This is the type of image spirit choose to show that they are perfectly at peace. He really is very happy and so very excited to be connecting with you."

Me "That sounds just fantastic!"

Juelle "He is telling me that you saved him and he is thanking you."

Me "Really, did I really? I always say that he saved me."

Juelle "He is also letting me know that he has had a bad experience in the womb in a past life, this wasn't with you, but with a different mother and he felt completely unloved and unwanted. He chose you in this lifetime to be his mum because he wanted to experience the opposite. He wanted to feel unconditional love. He chose you because of your beautiful qualities and because he wanted to know how it felt to be completely and irrevocably loved and wanted. You gave that to him, and he's so grateful, he is telling me that you saved him."

Me "That is so beautiful, and I feel that he saved me too. I only felt settled in this country after I discovered that he is with me. I sensed that something, that somebody, as it turned out, was missing from me and once I fully accepted his being around me, I finally felt restored. It was as if my soul knew that it was incomplete, so he, without a shadow of a doubt, truly saved me."

Juelle "He is asking me to let you know again that you did nothing wrong, nothing at all! This relationship is about Kieran's journey. He wanted to experience the warm, loving, light, blissful environment of the womb. He didn't need to stay for very long to gain such an appreciation, and he definitely didn't want to be birthed out into the dark, dense energy here on the earth."

Juelle then went on to explain that having come from the delightful realm of Heaven and all of the pure light and love enveloping souls there, and then moving into the nurturing loving surroundings of the womb, to continue on and to enter earth would have been a real wrench. Many spirits only require a very brief time on earth to complete a particular life lesson or to experience a certain aspect which was missing from their previous earthly incarnation. My son only needed to remain with me for a short (in earthly timing) period to gain what was required for him to continue to grow spiritually.

This explanation, encouraged me, for the very first time, to really look deeply at things from my son's perspective, rather than from my own. All along I had thought that losing my child was all about me, that I was the cause of his early departure, that his leaving must be a life lesson, (and a very cruel one at that) for me, but now I was being presented with a thoroughly eye-opening alternative! Had I processed this correctly? *Was the decision to leave Earth early in this lifetime, completely and unreservedly, entirely my son's?*

I have mentioned before that I've read that we each belong to a family of souls, who we then reincarnate with as various family members and friends, in further lifetimes. I have also read that we decide ahead of each reincarnation, some of the trials that we will experience in order to grow. Each member of the soul group is aware of their individual personal role, and an agreement is reached between the souls before entering the earthly plane.

My understanding is that, while a particular path is then expected to be followed, that there is also the option to follow a different path, leading to a new set of life lessons. I'm not sure how often this occurs, but you will have heard of the expression 'having free will,' and I suspect that this might come from a soul agreement not being set in stone.

With regard to my son, I wonder if we both previously agreed that he would only be on earth for a short time, or if his decision to leave was only made once he'd reincarnated. If this is the case, am I allowed to know why?

Juelle certainly seems to think that my son's lifetime was predestined, so I must presume that he only needed a very short earthly life this time around. I must have been one incredibly brave soul to agree to let him go!

Perhaps this is what was meant by me now being able to see the bigger picture. Would I have been selfish to deny my son his choice of a departure time from this plane? Maybe I would have caused him great suffering, by making him endure a lifetime here when he was destined to spend it in such a beautiful, light and love-filled place. If this is the case, then I will happily accept the pain caused by his absence, rather than force it onto my child.

I am certain that my son's messages are not unique to my situation, and that he is speaking on behalf of all precious angels. The overriding message conveyed is that we have nothing to beat ourselves up about. We are not to blame, in any way, shape or form, for our child's early departure from this dimension.

Juelle "The connection you share with your son, is not going anywhere, you will always be connected. He has so much love for you his amazing Mum. He loves and adores you so much, he thanks you and he isn't going anywhere. He asks me to tell you that he doesn't want you to join him for a long time yet, but one day, you will get to see him, to hold him and to be with him. He will be waiting for you. In the meantime, he asks me to tell you that he is with you in the everyday things. When you make a cup of tea, when you hang the washing on the line, when you cook the dinner, he is with you. He is never far, and he loves you so very much."

I felt incredibly moved by our conversation and then delighted when Juelle suggested that we do a guided meditation. She had asked my son if he would like to meet in the peaceful garden, we were last brought together in and was a little surprised I believe when Kieran suggested meeting at a beach instead.

He then went on to explain that he finds it most easy to connect when there is water around, and therefore recommended a place close to the ocean. I found this request very intriguing and, once Juelle had reassured me that she'd hold my son's energy throughout, to assist him in coming through strongly, off to the beach we headed!

Juelle *"You are walking along an empty beach, it looks just like one of the beaches on the west coast of Auckland."*

For those of you unfamiliar with the Auckland coastline, the western side consists of vast, wild, rugged and often black sand coated, beaches. The waves on such beaches are powerful, coming from the mighty Tasman Sea, yet the imagery and feelings conjured up at each of these stunning places are that of very natural unspoilt beauty and a tranquil, peaceful setting that very much speaks to the soul. I wasn't at all surprised when I discovered that this was to be our meeting place.

Juelle *"You are walking along the beach, barefoot, and are enjoying the feel of the sand beneath your feet. It is a warm day, not too hot, just a very comfortable temperature. The beach is deserted, and you continue walking along to the end of the beach until you are met by a collection of rocks, some are large, and others are smaller.*

As you move toward the rocks, you notice that a pool of sea water has collected in one of them. You step up onto a large rock which is higher than this one, take a seat on it and then dangle your legs down a very short way so that your feet are now resting in the pool.

You feel safe and relaxed and close your eyes, taking in the gentle breeze, the sensation of the warm water and the occasional sound of a bird taking flight. After a few moments, feeling completely calm and content, you open your eyes and see a figure approaching you from the midpoint of the beach.

As the figure draws closer, you realise that it is your lovely son. Once he has reached the rocks, you pause for a moment to take everything in and then invite him to join you in the rock pool. He sits down beside you, and you embrace. When you are ready, you begin chatting with each other. Perhaps you are now holding hands, and are exchanging loving messages to each other. You remain at the rocks for quite some time, and at one point, Kieran reaches down and picks up an object which he then hands to you.

Eventually, you know that it is time to part again, just for now. You step out of the water and down from the rocks and begin the slow walk back along the beach, the two of you side by side.

Reaching the far end of the beach, you make your preparations to leave. Embracing once more, and exchanging yet more loving words. You know that you can meet again.

But for now, it is time to exit the beach and to say farewell to each other. As you reach the edge of the sand, you turn to glance for a final time, and then your attention is drawn to the gift nestled in the palm of your hand. Smiling to yourself, you open your fingers and glance down at the treasure, a beautiful reminder of an incredible encounter."

Once I'd arrived back into full consciousness, we compared what we'd each seen. I commented on the fact that as my son and I moved back along the beach, I first tried to visualise him walking beside me, but was unable to do so and, instead, I saw him quite clearly, floating above the sand!

Not at a great height, but his feet were definitely not on the ground. He also moved exceptionally lightly.

Juelle nodded to me and said that she had seen the same thing and that he was floating as lightly as a feather and at high speed at times. We chatted further and discovered, even more, similarities with our recounts. I was then asked to select a crystal from a vast array sitting on a large shelving unit, to replicate the object I'd been handed on the beach.

I felt quite overwhelmed by the variety on offer, there were literally hundreds to choose from, but eventually, I selected one that felt 'right' and thanked Juelle for her very kind and totally unexpected gift. Once home, I looked up the meaning of the crystal I'd chosen, which was a Blue Quartz, and discovered the following facts:

Blue Quartz is a stress relief stone, it assists in the ability to reach out to others, and stimulates intuitive insight. It purifies the mental, physical and emotional bodies, and is a soothing and calming stone, bringing a relaxing calming vibe to any situation. It works on the throat and third eye chakras, and when tuning into the third eye, it can help one to connect to higher realms and work with ascended beings.

It brings great clarity to psychic visions and dream work. Many use blue quartz to cleanse the aura and to clear away the toughest energy blockages. It assists with communication, not only with others but also communication from the higher self to the 3D self.

Well, as you can imagine, of all the crystals I could have picked, I felt pretty pleased with myself for singling this one out, but perhaps the credit should go to Kieran? Most importantly, of course, I felt so blessed to have a physical reminder of the precious time spent on the beach with my son and will treasure my crystal forever.

As always, I felt amazing after the meditation and found myself instantly accepting that I was right there with my gorgeous boy. I cannot recommend participating in such an experience enough. It helps if you have somebody to narrate for you, but it is also entirely possible to direct yourself through a meditation like this. Try to be as relaxed as possible, and open to seeing, feeling and hearing whatever comes up, I'm sure that you too would find it a very healing activity to take part in.

CONCLUSION

The loss of a baby is something that forever changes a person.
There will never come a time when we won't yearn for those
missed hugs and kisses. We will always wonder how our little
angel might have resembled us, what they might have made
of their lives, and a thousand other considerations are never
far from our thoughts.

The loss of a life before it had even begun is an almost
incomprehensible concept, yet the bereaved parent has
endured the unimaginable and is still standing. We may
be completely unsteady and frequently collapse under the
weight of our broken hearts, but eventually, we get up again
and force one foot in front of the other. This is the way of the
warrior and what a formidable warrior is she or he who has
lost the most precious of gifts.

Against all the odds, this most invincible of parents
has fought back from an indescribable gut wrenching, all-
enveloping pain and somehow mustered up the courage and
the strength to keep going. This is bravery personified!

Although you cannot physically hold your child right
now, and the longing to touch, to see and to be with them

continues, I hope that my experiences have offered some comfort, hope and reassurance that they are still very much with you and always will be. The beautiful relationship you shared with your little one continues on in spiritual form. Your angel feels your love, he in return loves you completely and unconditionally and walks beside you every day.

If you feel able to open your heart and mind to the possibility of receiving signs, you may be very pleasantly surprised. Perhaps a message will come to you through a song, thought, or maybe, you might like to ask him to come into a dream. Alternatively, you might find each other in meditation.

Invite your child to send you something or to offer communication via yourself or a medium, and don't be too quick to dismiss things or to put it all down to having an overactive imagination.

Love and life continue eternally, and you will be reunited with your little one again. For those of us who believe in reincarnation, and there certainly seems to be a lot of evidence in favour of it, we can also take comfort from knowing that we will get to spend many more lifetimes with our little angels.

Please know that you are still a mother and still a father. Your lost child has never actually been lost at all, he just slipped away into another room, patiently waiting for you to process your grief a little, to release some of the torturous pain that has long since engulfed you, and to unburden yourself from the misplaced guilt and blame.

Now that you have made it through the stormiest of weather, your little one is more easily able to reach through the thin veil that causes the illusion of separation. Your child lives on.

Love endures all things, and the notion of death is absolutely no match for the indestructible, unconditional, everlasting bond created between a mother and her child. Love conquers all.

With much Love and Light,
Lorraine.

LIST OF ORGANISATIONS AND HELPLINES

NEW ZEALAND

Sands – Offer support to families who have lost a baby.
Email info@sands.org.nz
Phone 027 7105 130
Sands have support groups throughout New Zealand, including the following areas – Auckland and Northland, Waikato and Bay of Plenty, Hawkes Bay and Gisborne, Taranaki, Wanganui and Manawatu, Wairarapa and Wellington, Nelson and Marlborough, Canterbury, Otago, West Coast and Southland.

Miscarriage Support (Auckland)
E mail support@miscarriagesupport.org.nz
Phone 09 360 4034

Miscarriage Support (Wellington)
Website www.miscarriagesupport.org.nz

Baby Loss NZ

Address 6, Tanah Merah Drive,

Papakura,

Manakau 2110

Phone 09 298 9307

Other Helplines

Lifeline - Provide a free 24/7 Helpline

Call 0800 54 33 54 or 0508 82 88 65 (Suicide Crisis Line)

If an emergency call 111

Depression Helpline – Free Helpline

Call 0800 111 757

Anxiety Helpline – Free Helpline

Call 0800 2694 389

Youthline- Free helpline, text and counselling services

Call 0800 37 66 33

Free text 234

Email talk@youthline.co.nz

AUSTRALIA

Sands

Helpline 13 00 072 637

Email support@sands.org.au

Sands Australia has a network of groups in Victoria, Queensland, South Australia, Tasmania and Western Australia.

Sands also offers a support line for men who would prefer to speak to another male.

Bears of Hope (Formerly Pregnancy Loss Australia)
Offer support to families who have lost a baby
Call 1300 11 HOPE
Email contact@bearsofhope.org.au

Other Helplines

Beyond Blue – 24/7 Helpline
Call 1300 22 4636

Suicide Call Back number 1300 659 467
If an emergency call 000

Lifeline
Call 13 11 14

Men's Line
Call 1300 78 99 78

UK

Sands
Helpline 0207 7436 5881
Email helpline@uk-sands.org
Sands UK have numerous support groups in and around England, Scotland Ireland and Wales

Miscarriage Association
Helpline 01924 200799
Email info@miscarriageassociation.org.uk

Miscarriage Support NCT
The National Childbirth Trust offer support for women
suffering from miscarriage or stillbirth.

Helpline 0300 330 0700
Website www.nct.org.uk/miscarriage

Other Helplines

Samaritans - Free call from the UK 116 123
Free call from the Republic of Ireland 116 123 also
E-Mail jo@samaritans.org
If an emergency call 999

Cruse Bereavement
Helpline 0844 477 9400 Mon – Fri 9.30am-5pm
Email helpline@cruse.org.uk

British Association for Counselling and Psychotherapy –
provide a list of accredited counsellors in Britain. There is
also a Scottish equivalent called COSCA
Phone 0870 443 5219 9am-5pm
E-Mail bacp@bacp.co.uk

The Compassionate Friends - a charitable organisation
for bereaved parents, siblings and grandparents who have
suffered the loss of a child
Helpline 0845 123 2304
E-Mail info@tcf.org.uk

US

Share Pregnancy and Infant Loss Support
Phone 800 821 6819
E-Mail info@nationalshare.org

MISS Foundation- offer counselling to those who have lost a
child
Phone 602 279 6477
E-Mail info@missfoundation.org

HAND – Helping After Neonatal Death
PO Box 341, Los Gatos, CA 95031
Call toll-free 1 888 908 4263

Other Helplines

Lifeline Crisis Chat 24/7 Call 1 800 273 8255
If an emergency call 911
Crisis Text line - in a crisis text HELLO to 7417

ACKNOWLEDGEMENTS

There are many people without whom, producing this book would never have been possible, and I am so grateful to each and every one of you. I very much see the birth of this book as a collaboration, and I would especially like to thank the following gorgeous souls:

My Four beautiful girls, thank you for allowing your Mum to indulge her passion, even though the subject matter was challenging and it meant that I was ensconced in my office for hours on end. Thank you for your patience and for choosing me to be your Mother. I am truly honoured to have four such amazing blessings of daughters, and I love each of you with all my heart.

My husband, Mark, thank you for believing in me and for helping me to believe in myself. You constantly encourage me to go that bit further to expand out of my comfort zone. Your frequent word count updates and shouts of encouragement ensured that I didn't give up even when the going got tough!

My father, Brian, many thanks for listening to me and for not passing judgement, even when you must have felt compelled to speak out. I thank you for supporting me through this pretty exceptional time of discovery and for being the great dad that you are.

My wonderful family in spirit, thank you for taking the time to come through in my readings and for sharing such loving and inspiring messages. I am so proud to be related to you all, and you will never be forgotten.

Juelle Hunt, you have my deepest gratitude for aiding me through this incredible journey. You have allowed me to unburden, to express, to process and to release and you continue to do so. I cannot thank you enough for building such a beautiful rapport with my son and for delivering so many touching and enlightening messages from him.

To all of the wonderful light workers. I am so grateful for the information and messages of love you have brought through from the afterlife. You are fabulous souls. Keep shining!

And finally, to the two stars:

My beautiful Mum, Isobel, thank you for reassuring me that you are safe, well and happy. I am so very grateful for your continued efforts to connect and for the amazing information you have presented to the mediums. Thank you for your eternal love and guidance.

My darling son Kieran, where do I begin? Thank you, Thank you, and Thank you! I am still, to this day, completely lost for words whenever I stop to process the sheer enormity of this experience. I cannot begin to convey the depth of emotion I feel, but I will be forever in awe. I knew beyond doubt that we were going to be mother and son, yet your physical presence seemed to have eluded me.

Thank you from the bottom of my heart for your tenacity, for your determination and for your love. It must have been so frustrating for you, yet still, you persevered, and I will be eternally grateful for this. I am absolutely overjoyed that after all of these earthly years, your presence has finally been acknowledged. I love you with all my heart.